Sometimes
I Trip
On How
Happy
We Could Be

Sometimes I Trip On How Happy We Could Be

Essays

Nichole Perkins

GRAND CENTRAL
PUBLISHING

New York Boston

Grand Central Publishing
Hachette Book Group
1290 Avenue of the Americas, New York, NY 10104
grandcentralpublishing.com
twitter.com/grandcentralpub

First Edition: August 2021

Grand Central Publishing is a division of Hachette Book Group, Inc.
The Grand Central Publishing name and logo is a trademark of Hachette Book Group, Inc.

The publisher is not responsible for websites (or their content) that are not owned by the publisher.

The Hachette Speakers Bureau provides a wide range of authors for speaking events. To find out more, go to www.hachettespeakersbureau.com or call (866) 376-6591.

A previous version of "Prince's Girl" was first published in Buzzfeed, February 8, 2015.

A previous version of "The Life of a Succubus" was first published in BuzzFeed, October 7, 2014.

Library of Congress Cataloging-in-Publication Data
Names: Perkins, Nichole, author.
Title: Sometimes I trip on how happy we could be : essays / Nichole Perkins.
Description: First edition. | New York : Grand Central Publishing, 2021. |
Summary: "Pop culture is the Pandora's Box of our lives. Racism, wealth, poverty, beauty, inclusion, exclusion, and hope -- all of these intractable and unavoidable features course through the media we consume. Examining pop culture's impact on her life, Nichole Perkins takes readers on a rollicking trip through the last twenty years of music, media and the internet from the perspective of one southern Black woman. She explores her experience with mental illness and how the TV series Frasier served as a crutch, how her role as mistress led her to certain internet message boards that prepared her for current day social media, and what it means to figure out desire and sexuality and Prince in a world where marriage is the only acceptable goal for women. Combining her sharp wit, stellar pop culture sensibility, and trademark spirited storytelling, Nichole boldly tackles the damage done to women, especially Black women, by society's failure to confront the myths and misogyny at its heart, and her efforts to stop the various cycles that limit confidence within herself. By using her own life and loves as a unique vantage point, Nichole humorously and powerfully illuminates how to take the best pop culture has to offer and discard the harmful bits, offering a mirror into our own lives"--Provided by publisher.
Identifiers: LCCN 2021010633 | ISBN 9781538702741 (trade paperback) | ISBN 9781538702758 (ebook)
Subjects: LCSH: Perkins, Nichole. | African American authors--21st century--Biography. | African American women authors--21st century--Biography. | Podcasters--United States--Biography. | LCGFT: Essays.
Classification: LCC PS3616.E7465 Z46 2021 | DDC 810.9/896073--dc23
LC record available at https://lccn.loc.gov/2021010633

ISBNs: 978-1-5387-0274-1 (trade pbk.), 978-1-5387-0275-8 (ebook)

Book designed by Marie Mundaca

Printed in the United States of America

LSC-C

Printing 1, 2021

To Willa F. Perkins and Fannie Mae Puckett

To Prince Rogers Nelson

Sometimes
I Trip
On How
Happy
We Could Be

Fast

The worst thing a little Black girl can be is fast. As soon as she learns her smile can bring special treatment, women shake their heads and warn the girl's mother: "Be careful." They caution the mothers of boys: "Watch that one." When adult men hold her in their laps too long, it's because she is a fast-ass little girl, using her wiles. She's too grown. She tempts men and boys alike—Eve, Jezebel, and Delilah all in one—the click of her beaded cornrows a siren's call.

Fast girls ruin lives.

Even as a girl whose pigtails unraveled from school-day play, I was fascinated with sex and romance and why boys looked up girls' skirts and why people climbed between each other's legs. Why did fathers kissing mothers on the back of their necks make them smile such a soft, secret smile? Why did boys stand so close to girls in the lunch line? Why did my sister sneak her boyfriend over, even when she knew Mama had forbidden it?

Why did Mama tell my father, with her eyebrows raised, that the only book I'd read from the Bible was Song of Solomon? Yet I knew not to say anything, because being a girl and talking about sex would mean that I was fast, that I was trouble, that I'd end up with a baby before I finished school. I didn't want to be fast, but inevitably my experiences with sex and boys began early and I learned to keep them hidden away.

My memories of kindergarten are mostly fuzzy, but I remember eating green eggs and ham that my teacher used food coloring to dye, reading Sweet Pickles books, the boy who kissed every girl during nap time, and the two boys I kissed under the back porch.

The nap-time lover, an oak-brown boy made of angles, would wait until he was sure the teacher was gone, then make his rounds. He was a lousy kisser. He'd mash his mouth against ours, lips closed, twisting his head back and forth like the actors in the old black-and-white movies we'd watch with our grandparents. I'm not sure why he started kissing us, but we girls were supposed to keep our eyes closed and remain passive, even as giggles lifted our shoulders from thin foam mattresses. One day, he came around and I kept my eyes open. I wanted to know if he closed his.

He did not. We stared at each other until our faces softened into brown clouds; then he licked my mouth. Why did adults like doing this? It was too wet and smelled of peanut butter. To get revenge, I stuck my tongue into his mouth. Then we battled, our tongues bubbling saliva out of the corners of our sticky lips. I'm not sure what the prize was, but he finally pulled away and laughed before moving to the next girl. Based on the rounds of "Yuck!" and "Ew!" that followed, he tried to slip other girls his tongue with varying success.

Over the next few days, he started bringing a handkerchief to wipe his mouth between girls. There were fewer exclamations of disgust. I'm not sure if he stopped the wet kisses or if everyone became used to them. With me, his kisses began to taste like peppermint candy but remained sticky. We kept our eyes open. I put my hand on the back of his head once, like the women in those same old black-and-white films. He grunted softly, the sound you make when you're surprised nasty-looking food tastes good. His response scared me, but I liked it. At five years old, I already knew that if you liked what boys did too much, no one would like you. Girls called you names. Boys rubbed themselves against you while you waited for your turn on the monkey bars.

I never touched him with anything other than my mouth again.

I don't remember how he was caught, but the nap-time kisses stopped. I think I missed them. Taking the required nap became difficult, because I was tense, listening for the rustle that meant someone was moving from his blue-and-red mat.

I soon found myself under the back porch at home with one of the little "mixed" (now called biracial) boys in the neighborhood. He had an afro of loose waves, like Mr. Kotter from the TV show, and blue eyes that changed colors, especially when his white mother called him home. He never wanted to go. One day, she yelled his name, and he pulled me under my porch and stared at me. His breath did not smell good. It smelled of hunger, a stale metallic scent, but when he leaned in to give me a kiss, I accepted it.

I put my hands on either side of his face, and he did the same. We pecked at each other with our mouths, thumbs invading each other's eyes, as we tried to imitate adults. And then his neighbor showed up—another boy our age. He was brown like me, with hair that blended into his skin but filled with close waves his mother made sure he brushed down all the time. His eyes were the same color as his skin but with black-black lashes. Those eyes were wide as he breathed out that he was going to tell we were being nasty. I reached out and kissed him, too. I don't remember how he tasted, but I know he stopped talking.

I've lost track of how long we were under the back porch. The boys took turns kissing me. I took turns kissing them. My mother called me from the kitchen, and I hurried from our little cove. The boys' mothers would just yell and yell until they came home, but my mother would come look for me. I shot into the house. My heartbeat fluttered my shirt. I could smell those boys on me—the foreign stink of their spit and sweat a secret reminder of my adventure.

Boys were quiet when you kissed them. They didn't tease you for being skinny or bucktoothed or smart. Boys followed your lead when you kissed them. Boys let you rescue them from home when you kissed them. But kissing boys meant you were fast. Being fast meant you had babies nobody wanted and women talked mean about you. When you were fast, old men smiled at you with half of their mouths and invited you inside when no one else was home. Fast girls ruined lives. I didn't want to be fast. I wanted kisses that were secrets I controlled.

———

Teenage motherhood is nothing new to my family, but it's something my mother wanted to stop with her, as far as her two daughters were concerned. My sister, Izzie, is what Mama calls a pull-out baby. She was born almost two years before Mama's high school graduation. When my sister was a teenager, I saw a note Mama had written her: "Always use a rubber." I giggled at the word "rubber," such an old-fashioned term by then. Seven years separate me and my sister, and I'd been hearing Mama's voice deepen with warning for a long time: "Don't bring no babies home unless you can take care of them."

My sister developed early. Until high school, she was always the tallest girl in her class. Her curves constantly fought against the age-appropriate clothes Mama bought for her, but Mama knew how grown men could be, so she tried her best to keep Izzie a child as long as possible. Luckily, my sister went along with that plan. She's the sweet and obedient one. Perhaps that's a part of being the firstborn in the family. We have a younger brother, J, so that makes me the middle child, the baby girl. I'm my father's firstborn. I am a mess.

I was a scrawny child who always carried books around.

For a long time, my family called me Bugs, as in Bugs Bunny, because of my overbite. Family friends said I was cute, but it didn't seem like boys thought so. At least, the boys I wanted to like me never did. I've since learned this is how life is, but until junior high, I felt overlooked for the girls who already wore training bras, had professionally styled straight hair, and who boasted of boyfriends at other schools.

My sister came of age in the 1980s. Izzie watched all those Brat Pack movies—*Sixteen Candles*, *The Breakfast Club*, and *Pretty in Pink*, plus stuff like *Weird Science* and *One Crazy Summer*...and I watched right alongside her. I sat next to her and watched MTV until the music videos started to repeat themselves.

So I listened to these songs and watched the videos; I watched the movies and saw my sister clutching her hand to her chest because a white girl who sews her own clothes got to kiss the rich, popular guy. I saw teenage love played out as Forever Love, as overcoming class divides and teaching the rich kid that poor people are cool, too. I saw that white girls got to bring home boys and yell at their parents and be wanted, even if by someone undesirable. No adult was monitoring them to make sure they weren't tempting grown men. In the movies, no white girls were considered "fast." Instead, they were pressured to have sex, not stay away from it.

Black girls were tucked way in the back of the extras or in the second row of the dance number, their hair looking burnt from too much straightening, their makeup chalky, and with no love interest more significant than a dance partner.

There were plenty of sassy Black teenagers on television, in characters like Dee Thomas on *What's Happening!!* or Tootie on *The Facts of Life*. These girls always had a smart remark ready on their lips and got plenty of laughs, but just like in real life around my way, every crush they had led to lectures or scolds: "He's just using you." "You don't know any better." "Don't make any decisions you might regret."

Images of white girls in love came easily, but everywhere I turned, Black girls were warned.

In the fifth and sixth grades, school friends started to become pregnant. My mother wouldn't let me go to their baby showers. She said it would condone their situation, and she didn't want me to think it was okay to have a baby before I even got to ninth grade. These preteen moms looked like they were in high school, but they had boyfriends who should've been in college. The girls wore gold jewelry and had haircuts like women with real jobs—tapered in the back with curls crunchy from holding spray in the front. They had figures that betrayed their ages and minds and could barely solve word problems, and yet they were the ones labeled fast. And maybe they were. Maybe they'd felt compelled to race to catch up to their bodies and ended up at a finish line they didn't expect.

I remember one girl asking me why the grass was always wet in the morning. I replied, "It's dew," and she said, "No, it's clear." She thought I was talking about feces, as in "doodoo." And this was a child being blamed for her own middle school pregnancy.

I was not unaffected by my classmates' becoming pregnant

young, even as I remained fascinated by sex and love. I was scared. Teenage pregnancy was a family curse, and every time I looked in the mirror, wondering when my boobs and booty would come in, I worried it would happen because of "an accident." I was the only one of my friends who was shapeless and without a boyfriend, or even a boy I was talking to. The girls started making noises about introducing me to friends of their boyfriends, and it scared me. When sixth grade began to come to a close and my mom asked me about where I wanted to go for junior high, I told her I wanted to go to a magnet school. Mama assumed I wanted a more challenging curriculum, but in reality, I wanted to leave my friends behind. I was afraid that if I stayed with them, I'd end up pregnant, too, and as much I hated having my body policed by the elders in my community, I did not want to be fast either.

I wanted to be loved.

———

Shortly before my fifteenth birthday, my friend Tanya and I went to a bowling alley. This friend had boobs and booty, played basketball, got her hair done on a regular basis (in a salon, not at a beauty school!), and wore gold necklaces and rings. My mother didn't like her. She was too fast, too mature for me, but Tanya was pretty much the only close girlfriend I had at the time.

So Tanya and I went to the bowling alley. Later, I realized she had already made plans to meet someone there and my presence had served as a smoke screen for her mother. We were playing an arcade shooting game when two high school boys walked up to us. Tanya immediately abandoned the game for one of the guys, but I tried to keep playing. I was used to being ignored and didn't like wasting my time with small talk, so I kept my attention on the game.

The other boy finally spoke to me, a simple, bored, "What's up?" He sounded like he'd been the wingman for the other guy all of his life. I'd learn later that was true. The two were cousins, with this bored one being younger by a year or two. I looked up at him, saw he wasn't hideous, and said hi before returning to the game. My heart started jogging in place. Just from my quick glance, I knew he'd be The One, my first. It felt like the moment in *Dirty Dancing* when Baby sees Johnny back at the employee cabins, dancing and drinking, only this guy didn't have Johnny's swagger (no one does). I felt awkward and flushed. I wanted to impress him somehow, but my only talent was writing and I wasn't about to bust out a poem about my dead grandmother, so I focused on shooting zombies. I had terrible aim but could cuss out the undead like no one's business. As the video game reset, I looked up at him and his eyebrows were raised in grudging approval. Yes!

This guy I'll call Rocco—he wasn't the kind of handsome that could turn heads with the first look, but he was the prettiest color I'd ever seen, a red-gold-brown that sang whenever he wore deep colors like burgundy, navy, and hunter green. He had a wide face with sharp cheeks, and eyes that naturally slanted up and disappeared into those cheeks when he laughed. He had a full mouth with a contagious smile, but he was short and skinny and girls kept their distance.

He had no car, no job, no chain, and he went to a high school where all of that mattered. None of that was important to me. His skin and smile held my attention. And he was funny. He didn't have a lot of book smarts, but he liked to make me happy. After exchanging numbers at the bowling alley, we talked daily. My mother refused to let me have an official boyfriend until I was sixteen, so I lied about going to the movies with Tanya. Well, Tanya was there, making out with Rocco's cousin Dante, while Rocco and I made out, too. When school was dismissed for the year, Rocco enrolled in a summer camp a few blocks from where I lived. He'd walk down to my house after it let out, before my mother or sister got home, and we'd hang and kiss some more.

I liked Rocco. I think by the time summer was in full bloom, we were even telling each other "I love you," but my family's history of teen pregnancy loomed. Even my sister had succumbed to it, but she had choices our matriarchs didn't, so she followed my mother's rule and brought no babies home.

But honestly, more than the fear of continuing a family curse, I worried I'd like sex way too much. Here comes that fear of being fast again, but by this age, I wouldn't be labeled fast. I'd be called a ho. Hoochie. Skank. Skeezer.

At some point in July, about four months after Rocco and I first met, he finally turned up the heat and began to pressure me. He even offered the tired old sentiment that if I loved him like I said I did, I would go ahead and let it happen. I told

Rocco that if that's what he thought, then maybe we should stop seeing each other. He backpedaled, and we continued our relationship. Then the next month, It happened.

I still remember the exact date: August 3, 1992. I'm horrible with dates, but this I remember, probably because I wrote a poem[1] about it. The poem, recovered from an old hard drive somewhere, is as bad as one can imagine a teenager's poem about her first time to be. I described his fingers as cinnamon sticks, for Pete's sake, said he had "melted caramel" skin.

At the time, my sister, Izzie, a recent college graduate, still lived at home but was asleep in her room. Rocco had come by after his summer camp, and we started making out on the couch. This time, when he slipped his hand into my panties, I didn't stop him. I'd decided I was finally ready, and I wanted to reward him for staying with me after I'd made him wait.

---

1   I found the poem:

August 3, 1992

Hands the color of melted caramel
pour down my spine
molding against the tender
arch of my foot.
Whispered words of love and persuasion
part full soft confident
lips.
Fingers the length of cinnamon sticks
gently tease the doubtful
flesh of my thighs
while shocked gasps
are captured by a greedy
mouth.

At first, he was just rubbing along my skin. I raised my hips to guide him. I'd been masturbating since I was eight or nine, so at fifteen, I knew where and how I liked to be touched. He started to move his fingers in and out but met the resistance of my hymen. I remember holding my breath as he pushed through and broke it. It didn't hurt, like the books and general gossip had said it would. It felt like that frustrating moment when you get your arm stuck in a too-tight shirt, and as you struggle to correct yourself, one of the seams snaps loose. An internal seam had popped, and I thought, *That's it?*

We fooled around a bit more before he asked if we could go to my bedroom. I lightly called my sister's name, but based on the snoring coming from her room, I knew she would be asleep for a while. My brother and I had bunk beds, the ubiquitous red metal set, with the bottom bed a full mattress and the top a twin. Because I was older, I got the bottom bunk. The space between my bed and the underside of my brother's, already snug, grew smaller with Rocco on top of me. I wondered if this was what being in a coffin felt like.

As Rocco positioned himself more carefully between my thighs, I thought about my mother, then a nurse, and how she'd once described feeling her water break when she was pregnant with me. She had been folding laundry when she heard a soft pop, then felt a trickle of fluid down her leg. She'd told me my father's reaction, how he started to panic. Rocco, despite his trembling above me, managed to push himself inside, and there was the painful sting I'd been expecting. The condom made a weird slick sound as the air bubble Rocco had left cleared away. He started to move, and this was it. I was finally having sex. It wasn't so bad.

Even though I was a teenager when I lost my virginity, I still felt a small victory in waiting as long as I did. It was with someone I loved; it was a decision that wasn't taken from me; and there was no humiliating scene where everyone in school found out and tried to ruin my reputation. Because my first time was with someone I naïvely thought I would marry, I'd beaten the curse of being fast. I was already a bit of an unfashionable nerd, with horrible hair and terrible teeth, so I had none of the vixen-like characteristics that came with being fast. I had won.

I didn't have an orgasm that first time. I faked it, using old Prince songs as my guide, but quietly, since my sister was still asleep in her bedroom. Rocco came, of course, because he was a teenage boy having sex for maybe the second time in his life. He fell on top of me, his elbows going out, and buried his face in the pillow next to my ear, gasping and shaking as if he were dying. I loved it. There was a rush through me— a ticklish thrill I wanted to chase forever. In that moment, I felt powerful.

In that rush, I felt the real reason people hated "fast girls." They hated that these girls and young women knew the power of their bodies—and, in some cases, yes, exploited it. They hated that adults could be weak enough to prey on girls learning how to control that power. With Rocco a mess between my thighs, I felt like I could ruin his whole life if I wanted. There was no shame in this moment. No fear. No worry. I felt like a god.

The elixir of being fast was addictive.

————

By the time I was with my college boyfriend, DJ, I finally felt like all those romance novels I'd read were true. I would see him, and my stomach would flutter. We'd walk across campus toward each other, smiling the whole way. With my back to the door, I would know when he entered a room. When we had sex, he made me feel as weak as I made him feel. With DJ, I wanted to be a "good girl" to prove I was worthy of marriage, that I wasn't fast. He didn't want me to smoke or drink, so I didn't. I was smack-dab in the middle of New Orleans, throat as dry as death, just to prove I took his wants seriously. We explored many sexual firsts with each other, but they were mostly his firsts. As much as I wanted to do everything that made him think I was The One for him, there was always something in the back of my mind, telling me there was more to my life than being someone's Build-A-Wife project.

When I first saw DJ at the freshman welcome mixer, a voice went off in my head: *That's the man you will marry.* I was eighteen. That was still the secret expectation of college—get the education your parents couldn't have, but really, you're there to find your husband. I thought I had, but it became clear that in the eyes of our friends and classmates, I was not my own. I was simply "DJ's girl." Many of them literally called me Lil DJ. It began to chafe. I wanted more for myself, and DJ wanted more out of his life as well.

I'd spent my high school and college years, from Rocco onward, as a serial monogamist, hoping the shield of exclusivity would protect me from being called fast. Protect me from temptation, from ruining lives. In adulthood, the names for a sexually adventurous woman were worse, but I still wanted to explore the power I felt when men shook in my arms.

There was so much shame and secrecy about sex and its exploration, but I chose to lean in to the desires pulsing through me, and maybe that's what saved me.

A Woman Who Shouts

I was mad at God for a long time.

When I was a tween, I took romance novels to church and read them through sermons. When my mother made me put away those books, I read Song of Solomon in the Bible. There's no way that was about the love God had for His "bride," the church, with opening lines like "Let him kiss me with the kisses of his mouth! / For your love is better than wine." Who is asking God to kiss them on the mouth? And why? You're not even supposed to be able to look at the full glory of God without going insane or blind or something, but we're supposed to believe Song of Solomon is about God's love for his congregants and not about a man and a woman falling in love and doing The Nasty. Sure.

So I'd read Song of Solomon and learned erotic poetry when I should've been listening to the Word, which always seemed to be directed at the adults. Sunday school was the same old collection of stories I'd already learned through movies like *The Ten Commandments* and *Noah's Ark*. The boys got cool action stories about Moses parting the Red Sea, David killing Goliath, or Shadrach, Meshach, and Abednego walking in fire, but girls were warned not to be bad, like Eve ruining everything, Delilah ruining Samson, or Jezebel...also ruining everything.

As I got older, church never felt like it was for me. I hated the way my attire was monitored for appropriateness: "You need a slip on." "You need to put on some stockings." "Where's your shawl? You need to cover your shoulders." "Your skirt is too short." "Those earrings are too big." It's not like I showed up to church in a bikini, but I was a teenager, trying to assert myself in small ways and rebel against doing things just because that's the way it's always been.

Church was almost always the same: getting there early for Sunday school, suffering through one of the ushers who was trying not to fall asleep while teaching us about David and Goliath, then the actual service. The choir marches in. The pastor comes out and opens with a prayer, a reminder of what he hopes we'll accomplish in church that day. There are some choir selections, an offering, more prayer, more singing, another offering, announcements and recognition of guests, another song, then the pastor preaches something that's not for me before he opens the doors of the church, metaphorically welcoming anyone who is ready to give their lives over to God but especially to our church so we can have their tithes. After the sermon and call to worship, there's another song and prayer to seal in the effects, and then you can leave, but only after you've hugged everyone and made small talk with a bunch of people who wouldn't know how to spell your name if God came down and offered them the kingdom of heaven to get it right.

One of the lessons of Sunday school was that if you follow all of God's rules and all the instructions for prayers, you can have anything you want. God rewards the faithful. I'd head to the altar, bow my head, and pray according to the guidelines:

- Address God properly. *(Heavenly Father…)*
- Give thanks. *(Thank You for waking me up this morning.)*
- Acknowledge His bounty. *(I know You didn't have to. So many others did not see the sun today.)*
- Thank Him again for doing what He knows you're about to ask for. *(Thank You for blessing me with the money to pay next month's rent. I don't know where it will come from, but You will provide.)*
- Share God's blessings. *(I ask that You look out for my sister and bless her with the promotion she needs.)*
- Seal the prayer. *(In Your son Jesus's name…)*
- Close. *(Amen.)*

They say you're not supposed to ask for the same thing more than once, because it means you don't trust that God will take care of it. Maybe that's where I messed up. I repeated prayers, trying to let God know I was serious and to remind Him, in case He forgot about me. I kept asking for God to make my brother "normal," to make my father stop hitting my mother, to not let Muh'Deah or Gran'mama die. He ignored me, and I was angry.

I may have chafed against the structure of worship services and battled resentment for God, but I've always loved the history of my church. I'm AME—African Methodist Episcopal, a denomination officially founded in 1816 by a Black man named Richard Allen, who was tired of the segregation affecting churches. The unofficial roots go back even further, to 1787 with the Free African Society, which provided mutual aid services to freed Blacks in Philadelphia. I love being connected, however loosely, to people who saw a problem and created a solution that continues to thrive. My pride in the history of my denomination is part of what keeps me Christian. If my people can break away from the boundaries of racism, I can wear a T-shirt dress with tennis shoes and hoop earrings to church. That makes sense to me.

I did not enjoy the social rituals of church. My family's home church is small, and it was crucial to speak to and hug everyone after services were over. I'm a little "antisocial," as my family and childhood friends like to point out. Small talk drives me up the wall. I'm also particular about smells, so having to hug everyone and get their scents on me—ranging from "too much perfume" to "too much cologne"—irritates me. As soon as I got to my messy teenage years, I'd try my best to meet societal expectations by waving to people as I bolted to the car to wait for the rest of my family.

The best part of church was, of course, the singing. Our church choir wasn't stellar and was too small to do big gospel numbers with rounds and intricate arrangements, but they did their best and I always paid attention to the selections. If you ask a Black person deep in Black church politics, they'll tell you AME churches are quiet and "bougie," which means we don't do all the hooting and hollering people associate with Black churches, especially Black Baptist churches. We don't speak in tongues. There won't be anyone running circles around the pews. No one falls out. Well. People do catch the Holy Spirit, and there is some shouting, a little hot-stepping, maybe some other kind of carrying-on. Usually when people start shouting, an usher will immediately head over to them and start fanning them down. Can't get too excited in the name of Jesus.

There was one time I thought I was about to catch the Holy Ghost. The choir was performing with a special guest, someone who frequently stopped by to play the piano and lead the choir. V had a rich, smoky voice that should've been backing Aretha Franklin, Chaka Khan, or Mariah Carey, if not having her own career. When V sang, it made all the clothing criticism I'd get worth it. V always sang like she'd burst if she didn't release whatever was inside her. People joke that when Anthony Hamilton sings, a pot of greens magically appears in your kitchen. When V sang, it was like nursing a glass of whiskey while a brokenhearted woman let go in a juke joint. In church, even her joy had edges.

I don't remember what song she sang, but I had my head down, eyes closed, really listening. A chill started at the back of my neck. Not the kind that makes you say "Someone just walked on my grave." That's a fleeting sensation that makes you shake your body to brush it off. No, this tingling sat at the top of my spine, waiting for me to notice it, and when I did, it traveled up until my scalp felt like it was shimmying around my mind. I thought I heard a deep voice, which sounded like it was smiling at me, say "I'm here," and it scared me so much I opened my eyes and sat up in my seat. I was still a teenager when this happened, and the fear of becoming a woman who shouts made me leave the sanctuary and go outside.

I hated church, didn't I? I hated sermons about being a virtuous woman and what a prize one is to her husband. I hated being nice to people who thought my mama was stuck-up and therefore her children were, too. I hated the sermons that never held anything for me and yet I was supposed to praise the pastor. No one could tell me why it had to be that way or why I had to follow certain rules other than tradition.

I couldn't become a woman who shouts. God didn't listen to me. As a child, I prayed all the time with all the passion I had, and still my grandmother was gone. She was my father's mother and gave me Juicy Fruit chewing gum every time I saw her, and she always smiled at me like she'd been waiting for me her whole life, and she was gone. Even now, I want to call up memories of her, but she is fading, her body a wispy blur moving through the images of her living room, her kitchen, sitting in her bed when cancer had weakened her. I never even knew she was sick until she was gone. Mama said I was too little to go to her funeral, but my younger cousin went, and I was mad at God for that, too. How could God be real, how could He be a being we should praise without question when He took Gran'mama away before I could seal her voice, her face, to her memories?

I had so much anger in me toward God, and I couldn't tell anyone, because if you said you were mad at God, it meant you were the devil—or worse, you had to talk to the pastor. I didn't want parables about children honoring their parents or the rod or prodigal sons. I wanted my grandmother and my great-grandmother, who raised my mother and hated my father but loved us children with incredible food and soft white bedsheets and heavy pink soaps. I wanted my brother to go back to being "normal" so my mother could catch a break and have one less worry. I wanted us to have a house free from rats and the constant need of repair. I wanted to talk about the fire inside me that made me crave touch and sighs without someone warning me I was going to hell. God said no, no, no, so why was He here, a voice along the curve of my neck and nothing more?

I stepped into the parking lot, and I was scared. I hoped God wasn't trying to recruit me. I could not be a preacher. My blood runs too hot, and even though I'd just started having sex when this... spiritual contact happened, I knew I didn't want to give it up in order to consecrate myself to God's mission, or whatever it was He might have wanted me to do. I watched clouds move across the sky, hoping to calm down, and hoping for a clearer message about what God wanted from me, because if that was a call to preaching, I had to reject it. Would God be mad at me now for rejecting Him? Would He send more heartache my way?

I sat on the church sidewalk, asking myself questions like this, and it didn't really soothe me. I started to worry, until I realized maybe God didn't want anything from me at all. Maybe He just wanted me to know He knew who I was. As soon as that thought appeared, I felt calmer. Maybe not at peace, like I had divine knowledge, but it seemed like that was the answer and it was enough: I think I needed to know God knew I existed. Church made me feel lonely, but that sprinkle of the Holy Ghost let me know God knew me.

He didn't offer me anything, and my life didn't become immediately better after all of this. I didn't start proselytizing. I still hated the social obligation of church, and I couldn't wait to get away from home for college so I could avoid it without anyone making me feel bad. (I ended up at a school that made us attend chapel every Tuesday during our freshman year.) College magnified the hypocrisy of Christianity. I learned about the pagan rituals folded into the religion to make it more palatable as people were forced to convert, like the meanings behind Easter eggs and Christmas trees. I'm not going to get all sophomore year here, but I was the college-educated cliché, rejecting the structure of religion, even as I knew I still believed in a higher power. I mean, I honestly don't understand why God and evolution can't exist at the same time.

Years later, when I lived in Los Angeles, I felt very lost and wanted…something. I don't know what I was looking for, but I joined an AME church with great historical significance to Black LA. Going to church again gave me something to look forward to. The sermons finally made sense to me. I even attended Bible study and bought CDs of church services that really spoke to me. Barack Obama made the church one of his campaign stops during his first run for president of the United States and brought Stevie Wonder with him. And I was there! I was able to witness a part of history in a loving community attached to a Black legacy I felt so proud of.

I even got baptized! Mama went against tradition and did not have us children baptized as babies. She said she wanted us to make our own decisions about our commitments to God. I've always appreciated that, because I would've felt even more conflicted about my complicated relationship with God if I'd been forced into a promise I didn't understand the weight of.

When I worked at a nonprofit job, one of my supervisors, Maria, was a woman who kind of adopted me as a sister-friend and helped me find an affordable apartment. She was pretty devout and often asked me to attend church with her. I was a little hesitant, but she assured me it would be the thing I needed. The church was deep in South Central LA, and it felt like a revival inside an old storefront. There were no pews. Everyone sat on a folding chair or stood, because it was so crowded. The pastor and his congregants spoke in tongues when the Spirit moved them, and one time the pastor prophesied over me, meaning that I stood before him, he placed a hand on my shoulder, and he predicted my future in front of the whole congregation. This was not the structured AME church I was used to, at all, and I wasn't fully into it, to be honest. The revival feel made me think of a cult, but I guess any religion is a cult, so perhaps I shouldn't stick my nose in the air.

I didn't attend this church often with Maria, but one day, she told me the pastor was going to be baptizing people at Dockweiler Beach (the beach where all the Black people went) and she asked if I wanted to get baptized. I'm not sure she expected me to say yes, since I'd been dodging other services, but I surprised myself. It felt like it was time. I could've elected to get baptized at the AME church I was attending, but there was an entire production behind it, and I didn't want to do it in front of everyone there. Plus getting baptized in the ocean sounded cooler—somehow more significant.

On the way to the beach, I started feeling a little panicky. I can't swim well. These people, the church members who'd be holding me, were strangers. What if this really *was* a cult? I wore a plain one-piece swimsuit under my clothes but had an extra outfit in my bag. When we got to the beach, I thought about walking away and getting lost in the crowd. I'm not really sure why in this fantasy I would have had to become a fugitive if I didn't get baptized, but that's how my anxiety was manifesting.

The beach was pretty crowded, bringing on the added stress of so many people watching me during a somewhat intimate moment, but I convinced myself that maybe none of the people in the crowd would be paying any attention to us. And that's exactly what happened. We church folks left our bags on the beach and walked into the ocean. We didn't go very far. Sand was always under my feet, until the moment the pastor coaxed me into bending backward, the sounds of his prayers muffled against my heart's thrashing and the water's lapping against me. I don't remember what he said over me, but I remember rising from the water, eyes closed tightly so I wouldn't lose my contacts, and feeling…no different. I'd wanted a big spiritual sign, like I'd look up into the sky and God would give me a thumbs-up and then I'd start to levitate, but no. I seemed to be the same.

What I remember most clearly is standing under the shower next to the restrooms and a woman from the church, who was there as witness, walked up to me and said, "You have such a glow about you. You have been anointed, do you know that? God pays special attention to you." I didn't know what to say to that, especially since she was not the first person, at this church or in my life overall, to have told me something along those lines. It didn't really feel like I was special to God, considering how much I disliked church and how angry I was at Him for causing so much pain in my family's life. I smiled at her and told her thank you, but I didn't go back to that church again.

And then something happened that left me fully dis-illusioned with churches and relying on men to interpret the word of God. The pastor of my AME church was accused of embezzling money, even transferring ownership of the low-income housing and other nonprofit entities from the church to his wife, and having an affair with another pastor. It was the height of the 2007–08 recession, and I was working various educational nonprofit jobs, which meant I was making dust as a salary. I would tithe and sometimes give the last of my money, literally nickels and pennies, to the church. Things were so tight for me financially that I actually went to one of the church's food drives in order to get groceries, but I felt so ashamed at being a single, child-free woman in need of help when the line was full of families and the elderly that I left without food. All the while, the pastor was (allegedly) spending church funds on jewelry, excessive trips, clothes, and more.

I stopped going to the church after the accusations came out. More than betrayed, I felt ashamed. Megachurches have a reputation of being ATMs for greedy pastors, and I had been naïve to think this one was different. The situation made me doubt God again. Why did He allow so many charlatans to benefit from His Word? How could I learn if all the teachers were corrupt? I had fallen for one of the oldest grifts known. I'd thought I was smarter than that.

When the pastor's alleged misdeeds came to light, no one in the congregation seemed to talk about it. Everyone was in a state of shock. In the last Bible study session I attended, I asked, "How could he do that?" One of the elders shook his head, his eyes on the table, and said, "The Lord will deal with him." The answer didn't satisfy me. I didn't want revenge, but I knew the church would no longer be a place of community and strength for me. My shame and betrayal had turned to anger. I couldn't figure out what lesson I was supposed to have learned. It seemed like yet another example of Trust No Man.

I pray in bed now—in the morning when I open my eyes, and at night when I close them for the day. I pray when I see 11:11 come up on clocks because maybe an angel is keeping watch. When my rent check clears, and I log out of my banking app, I whisper, "Thank You, Jesus." I don't go to church at all anymore. God knows how to find me.

Kermit the Frog

When I was a little girl, I had a lot of Miss Piggy stuff. I remember most vividly a white sweater with her in a hot-air balloon shaped like a heart. I used to walk around the house, doing little karate chops, backhanding imaginary people, and yelling out "hiiiYAAAH!"—like Miss Piggy whenever she saved the day or needed to get rid of someone who was working her nerves. After I graduated from college, I took a karate class for the summer and my mother remarked, "Well, you finally get to be Miss Piggy, don't you?"

I connected with that felt porcine femme. She was stubborn, bossy, and passionate. She loved Kermit, and Kermit loved her back. His frowns and exasperated sighs went along with all the other images of put-upon men in relationships, like Mr. Furley from *Three's Company* or Archie Bunker on *All in the Family*. The world kept telling me that men, even as frogs, hated relationships, especially with women, and they tolerated both because they had no choice. The way to a man's heart was to wear it down.

Kermit didn't even have anyone else he was interested in. He had too much on his plate as the logical Muppet, the leader, the one who tried to keep all the other creatures from getting into shenanigans. Honestly, it doesn't even matter why he didn't want to be with Miss Piggy. She refused to take no for an answer, vacillating between high-pitched baby talk and snuggles to woo him and backhanding him through walls when he refused her. As a child, I laughed along. Miss Piggy's mood swings and violence were supposed to be funny. If nothing else, they were familiar.

———

My father drank and did drugs. He couldn't (or wouldn't) hold a job, resentful that someone as intelligent as he, even without a college degree, would have to do manual labor to make a living. My mother was the breadwinner. After my mom had my brother, J, the last of her three children, she tried to be a stay-at-home mother, hoping that would force my father to get a job and provide for the family. It didn't work. We remained in the projects, living on government assistance, until my mother went back to her old job as a dialysis nurse. Around the time my brother turned two, he was diagnosed on the autism spectrum. Mama knew she needed help to make sure my brother had the resources he would need; meanwhile, my father blamed her for making his son "retarded," for ruining the legacy of his name.

My father would beat my mother. I don't know when he started. It was long before my brother and I came along. My sister, Izzie, has a different father, and mine, in his drunken rages, would express all manner of jealousies about Mama's previous relationships. If my sister tried to stop him, he'd sneer, "What're you gonna do? You gonna call H? You think he can save you?" He never beat me or my sister, but he would be so mean with the belt to my brother when he misbehaved. I don't know if he thought whooping J would make him "normal," but it was terrible to see.

My mother's hard work plus the help of a relative on my father's side pulled us out of the projects and into a three-bedroom house in North Nashville, a working-class neighborhood. My father's violence and addiction came along. One night, I watched him punch my mother so hard she flew backward across the room. Her fall broke the coffee table. I'd stubbed my pinky toe on that table once, leaping from chair to couch, and my toenail had fallen off. I hated that table, mad that it had ruined my flight. I used to wish I were magic so I could make it disappear. Watching my mother land on top of it, seeing it break beneath her weight, my father hovering over her, his face red and sweating, I was mad all over again. Why couldn't I have made it disappear or even better, made a portal appear, a gateway to safety for all of us?

My father went to jail that night. When he got out and came back home, he pulled me into his lap and explained how much he loved my mother, even though sometimes she made him angry. So you see, I was used to seeing someone use love to send the object of their affection through walls.

————

I would eventually realize how abusive the relationship between Kermit and Miss Piggy was. In 2011, I went to see Jason Segel's revival movie *The Muppets* and almost cried at how peaceful it felt seeing the pair appear on-screen. The Muppet characters made me remember what it was like when all I had to worry about was how many bowls of Toasted Oats (the Kroger store brand of Cheerios) I could eat. Then Miss Piggy began exhibiting her jealousies. As an adult woman, I saw her issues magnified. She craves attention and flirts wildly, but if Kermit even talks to a female Muppet, Miss Piggy flies off the handle. Kermit is sensitive and thoughtful but walks on eggshells. He is afraid of her. He gives in to her demands to avoid her anger and violence.

I think of Kermit when I find myself spiraling, wondering why an ex refuses to love me the way I love him. When I find myself thinking, *I can make him love me*, I see Kermit's lips folded in frustration, his cute little Muppet face shaking as he tries to keep Miss Piggy's anger from rising. It may be a little silly to think of a child's puppet in the middle of a lovelorn breakdown, but it's my way of remembering that forcing myself on someone is violence in and of itself. I've had enough of that.

———

I haven't always calmed myself down. I've been stupid and petty, leaving high-pitched voicemails, hoping to coerce a response. No felt or cotton here, but I've offered the softness of my body to avoid rejection. I have relished the glint of fear in an ex's eyes as he glances around, wondering if I will cause a scene if he doesn't come home with me. I am not perfect. Unlearning this kind of manipulation is a process, but thank God for the magic of maturity and self-awareness, portals of safekeeping that finally did appear.

Miss Piggy still speaks to me—a passionate woman who knows her talents should be recognized—but Kermit is the totem I use when a broken heart tries to tell me I am my father's child.

The Women

Muh'Deah with Her Hair Down

Muh'Deah, my great-grandmother, ate onions and tomatoes like apples. She pressed money, wrapped in aluminum foil or Kleenex, into your hand as you were leaving her home. She kept candy in the trunk of her car, and if you were good in church, she'd walk you to that treasure chest and let you pick a few pieces. Muh'Deah would comb my hair, using a pink Goody brush with white bristles. She had old people's strength, the kind that came from years of raising seven children plus doing farmwork, then domestic work. She'd pull my hair into a ponytail so tight I'd have a look of constant surprise for at least a day.

Muh'Deah's favorite color was red, and it became mine, too. We'd sit in front of her large floor-model TV—the kind with the knobs that thunk-thunked when you turned them—

34

and she'd brush my hair into that death-mask ponytail while reruns of *Gunsmoke* or *Bonanza*, *The Big Valley* or *The Rifleman* ran in the background. I had a book of fill-it-in word puzzles. She'd give me a red-ink pen, slim and striped like a piece of peppermint candy, and keep half an eye on me as I connected words together. I'd show her my completed puzzles, and she'd say, "That's good, baby," before she touched my shoulder to signify she was done with my hair. It wasn't until I was an adult that I learned Muh'Deah couldn't read. I like to imagine that seeing me work those puzzles made her proud.

My memories of what Muh'Deah looked like are cloudy. My mother says that by the time I was born, Muh'Deah wore her hair short, just under her ears, but I remember something different. Once, I saw Muh'Deah with long hair—a braid that rested curled on her chest.

Muh'Deah lived in one of those senior citizen complexes that looked like a tropical vacation resort. It was late evening, and I was in the living room, fresh from a bath, smelling like Camay soap. I smelled good and had a belly full of biscuit and jelly. I was waiting on Muh'Deah to finish getting ready so I could use the mini steps that led to her four-poster bed, so thick and fluffy. Even though Muh'Deah would warm the bed with her onion-and-tomato-fueled gas, floating on the cloudlike mattress made it worth it. So there I was, fidgeting, trying not to ask if she was ready yet when someone knocked on the door. I froze in place. I knew I couldn't answer it. It was nighttime and no one visited Muh'Deah except family.

She came from the back of her apartment, wearing a long

white cotton gown. She didn't have her glasses on. And her hair...An unfinished braid lay against her right shoulder. If my eyes hadn't fallen out of my sockets from all those too-tight ponytails, surely they would fall out now. I think I even stopped fidgeting, and I know I stared in that openmouthed, uncaring child's way.

Muh'Deah answered the door, and it was one of her neighbors. A man. His glasses were so thick I couldn't really see his eyes clearly, but they were watery and shiny. He smelled like mouthwash but...more. Muh'Deah's mouth pulled into a tight line, which I would see on my own mother in later years. She invited the man in and let him sit on the couch, closest to the lamp with the bright, bright bulb. She sat in a chair and would occasionally give me The Look that meant I better behave, but she didn't send me to her room, out of the way, which is what usually happened when grown folks visited.

I have no sense for how long they talked. Muh'Deah touched her braid and finished it. I watched, fascinated. Then I noticed that Mr. Neighbor Man was also staring. Muh'Deah's fingers, taut with age and strength, moved quickly, working her hair into a simple plait, while she tried to remain polite. Suddenly, she dropped the completed work and made moves to stand. Mr. Neighbor Man struggled to be gentlemanly, despite his arrival without notice, despite his more-than-mouthwash smell, and helped her. Again, I can't remember what Muh'Deah said, but she ushered him out and made sure to set the locks on the door.

After wiping my face free of any more biscuit-and-jelly

crumbs, Muh'Deah pushed me down the hallway to her bedroom, hand on my shoulder. She made me say my prayers, then held on to my arm as I climbed into her bed. It was a child's heaven—all white sheets, a thick cushy mattress, with equally fluffy pillows and comforter. And full of love. The kind of love that leaves you with your eyes wide, that shares colors with you, that encourages you to be more than she could, and the kind of love that lets you protect her as she protects you.

Conversations over Lunch

"Nicki!" my mother yelled from the living room, even though my bedroom was directly next to it.

"Yes?" I yelled right back.

"C is on the phone!"

"Which C?"

"Come and get this damn phone!"

When I answered the phone, it was my aunt C, my father's older sister, with her deep but somehow lilting voice. She wanted to know if I'd like to go to the bookstore with her and maybe do some shopping, and we made arrangements for the next weekend. I was eleven or twelve, and back then, malls were still home to my favorite places, bookstores, especially the malls in white neighborhoods.

This was also around the time my mom finally kicked my dad out. My father had been arrested while driving Mama's car, the only working car we had, and it was impounded. That was the last straw. He said he'd been pulled over for running a yellow light, and maybe that was true, but what was definitely real and true was the fact that the police found drugs on him. Getting the car impounded had a direct influence on Mama's ability to get to work and, therefore, her finances, always tightly budgeted, and so she refused to deal with his sloppy irresponsibility anymore.

For a long time, I resented that she'd waited until a car was the victim of my father's mistreatment before she ended their relationship. He'd been such a terrible husband and father. It wasn't until I was older that I realized Mama thought a bad father was better than no father at all, because that's what she had experienced. She never knew who her father was, never had that relationship, but as many of us grow to learn: a raggedy piece of something is rarely better than the healthy whole.

———

My aunt C realized I needed a little escape from all the tension of my parents' divorce. My parents had put me in the middle of their issues. I'm my father's first-born, his parents' first granddaughter. My father couldn't have the relationship he'd expected with my brother, so he paid more attention to me. My mother frequently sneered at me about favoritism and fairness, because it was obvious I was my father's favorite. When my parents split, my father stalked my mom. When my brother and I visited him, he'd only ask questions about Mama—who she was seeing, was she going out at night, that kind of thing. He wasn't really concerned about us as his children, just as informants. Mama resented me because...I don't know. No, I do know, but it's hard to say your mother was jealous of you.

My father was never mean to me. He'd lie and steal from me, but he always showed me affection and never threw me across the room in a paranoid, drunken rage. Not that Mama wanted me to be on the receiving end of said treatment; she was always very protective of us children in that way and defended us. She once told me she was so happy to be pregnant with me because she thought it meant my father would start to act right. Yet when I came along, it didn't stop. I wasn't the cure. And it always bothered me that my father didn't love *any of us* enough to stop drinking and doing drugs and abusing her. This has led to a lifetime of worry that I'll never be enough for the good parts of love.

I think C understood more than I knew at the time. She's the oldest of my grandparents' four children. I later discovered that Gran'mama had been pregnant with her before she and Gran'daddy were married, and Gran'daddy resented his shot-gun wedding. He was cold to C as a child, ignoring her attempts at affection, and distant to my grandmother, blaming her for forcing them to marry. I don't have details, but I can imagine C wanted to offer me something she didn't have—a chance to get away from it all.

———————

C is the aunt who lives in the deep suburbs, close enough to be near family but far enough that there are no surprise visits. For as long as I can remember, she has been the Unbothered Auntie. She sees the family drama and will roll her eyes, let out a disgusted "ooh," and then go home to her peace. She drives with both feet, because driving makes her nervous, and she needs both feet ready to press the brake in case shit gets real. She is very fair-skinned and curvy in the way that's hidden by her cardigans and tennis shoes but makes country men extra polite. She always has her hair in a short but stylish cut, low and curly, the favorite of Black women who are tired of doing their hair but still want to look good. I don't think I've ever seen her in makeup. Her whole vibe has always said, "This suits me, and if it doesn't suit you, that's fine—I can go home." I love her.

C started picking me up every month or so. She'd take me to the fancy malls, Green Hills near Vanderbilt and CoolSprings Galleria in Franklin. The first time she took me to Davis-Kidd Booksellers, an indie specific to Tennessee, in Green Hills, I think my eyes fell out of my head. I'd been in bookstores and libraries before, obviously, but this was different somehow. The store itself seemed huge. People were everywhere. There was a café inside, and even though I have never liked coffee, there's something so welcoming about knowing you can be in a bookstore long enough to sit and have a hot drink.

C wanted to know what kind of books I liked, and when I

asked where the romance section was, she didn't roll her eyes or sigh. She led me there while making recommendations of authors she liked. Butterflies probably erupted from my head. We separated for a bit while she went to find her own selections, and when we reconnected, I had a stack of expensive hardbacks and the goofiest smile on my face. She went through my stack and said gently, "Let's find paperback versions of these," and we did. As I put back books we couldn't find, she replaced them with others she thought I might like. During a time when it felt like no one paid attention to me except to make me feel bad or tell me I was a reminder of someone who hurt them, here was someone opening new worlds to me.

———

Shopping with C was a lesson in retail etiquette. If a salesclerk was rude, she'd let out this very disgusted, very southern-lady high-pitched "ooh!" that means "I can't believe anyone on this earth has such terrible manners! I hope never to see you again!" When you make this sound, you have to pull one shoulder into your body, as if to say you must hurry away from this person before their rudeness becomes contagious, and also make your eyes go big in disbelief. She always did it as the person was walking away but still close enough to hear it, and we usually had no further problems. That "ooh!" is meant to make them think about how they were raised. I still use it.

After we finished shopping, we'd grab lunch. I'd try to

be conscious of money and say the mall food was fine, but we'd almost always end up at a nice restaurant. I'd tell her about school, and then we'd talk about movies and books. My house was always filled with pop culture. Someone's television or music was always going. Mama kept subscriptions to all the Black magazines, but it was with C that the discussions got real deep. C and I talked about camera angles and color schemes, allusions, metaphors, and symbolism. These conversations over lunch planted the seeds that would grow into my culture criticism career.

My sister and I watched *Cat on a Hot Tin Roof* with Paul Newman and Elizabeth Taylor every time it aired on AMC, back when AMC ran old movies with no commercials. We got a VHS copy of the movie so we could watch it whenever we wanted. We laughed at the accents and quoted unintentionally funny moments to each other, like when Big Mama was trying to make sense of Big Daddy's medical diagnosis and asked, "Well, what's wrong here?" For my sister and me, the film was a source of amusement and Paul Newman thirst, but when I watched it alone, I saw things between the lines, so I asked C about them. Was Newman's character, Brick, supposed to be gay? Was he in love with Skipper, his football teammate who'd died by suicide? C gave me Tennessee Williams's backstory and Hollywood gossip about Elizabeth Taylor, and we talked about the importance of lies and fertility in southern culture.

"Well, you know, Nicki," she started off, shifting in her chair at whatever casual dining restaurant we were at. She looked around to see if anyone was listening to us. "People like to keep their secrets."

I nodded my head, chewing on a Caesar salad with too much mayonnaise in the dressing. I didn't want to appear too eager, but I had a feeling she was thinking about her own secrets or something in our family.

"Families always want a lot of babies, especially boys, to carry on the name, and for *Cat on a Hot Tin Roof*, it was also about money. Maggie hadn't had any kids yet, so everyone thought something was wrong with her. Women have to have a lot of babies to be worth anything."

We both let that last sentence sit on the table between the salt and pepper shakers. C had only one child. Mama had told me she'd had a difficult pregnancy and birth, but no details beyond that. Her sister, my other aunt, who passed away when I was in college, had been trying to get pregnant for a while and was also having "difficulties." This was the first time that I worried about my own fertility.

"So in this movie, Nicki…" C picked up her critique, voice a little louder than she'd intended. She cleared her throat and resumed her previous quiet tone. "Maggie has to prove her worth to the family, especially since she didn't come from wealth, like Brick did. Basically, everybody has a past, and if they can't lie about it, they have to cover it up with something like marrying for money and status."

That made sense. Mama was always telling me I had to marry a rich man.

"Right," I said, "and everyone was hiding something, like

they were all lying to Big Daddy about his cancer." It was important to me that C knew I was following along. I wanted her to be proud of me.

"Mm-hmm, but if you ask me, Maggie should've left. Nobody wants to deal with all that mess," she said, and laid her fork on her plate. It seemed to signal both the end of the discussion and whatever memory was playing inside her own head.

———

C may have been the Unbothered Auntie, but she was also very private. One time, she told me how much she loved dark-skinned men, and she made a different kind of "ooh!" sound then, the kind that comes with a full-body shudder of delight. It was the first time I'd heard her talk about men without sounding annoyed. She was divorced by the time we started our Saturday excursions, and every now and then she'd tell me about a man she was dating, but it was always after the relationship was over and he'd been acting a fool. Her patience was thin for foolishness. She'd reached a point in her life where you had to improve it or leave her alone.

She taught me so much.

Our Saturdays continued faithfully throughout my teen years and into my early twenties. I'd talk to her about my boyfriends, and she'd punctuate their bad behavior with the disgusted "ooh!" she saved for retail workers. More than once, she'd say, "I don't know about him, Nicki," and shake her head over her salad.

Years later, I quit my first attempt at grad school and got a job at my college alma mater as a freshman advisor. The salary wasn't much, but it was my first real job that wasn't in customer service, and I was able to afford my first solo apartment. Still, I didn't feel like an adult until the Saturday I went home for a visit and asked C if she wanted to go to the mall and have some lunch. She picked me up as usual, and I filled her in on my relationship with DJ (broken, awkward, but I was enjoying single life) as she drove at a reasonable pace in the right lane of the interstate all the way across town. When we got to the bookstore, we split up and I made sure to get in line and buy my own books. I wanted her to see I didn't need her to buy everything for me anymore. I wanted her to be proud of me, Nicki the Adult. I wanted her to know that I enjoyed her company, that she wasn't just Auntie Moneybags. We went to a restaurant and I picked up the check. She said, "Well, thank you, Nicki," pleased as punch, the deep singsong of her voice making my name into a gold star.

My Sister's Bedroom

Izzie was in her bed, on her belly but raised on her elbows, reading a book out loud. As I walked farther into the room, I saw she had a small rectangular frameless mirror between her face and the book. She was watching her mouth move as she read.

"*What are you doing?*" I put every inch of disbelief and horror in my eight-year-old body as I could into the question.

"Get out of my room," she said in the same newscaster voice she was reading in. I got close to her and poked her in the arm. She always complained my skinny fingers hurt, so I was always poking her.

"Mama! Come get Nicki!" my sister yelled, and I frowned.

"You always telling on me," I hissed back.

"What is she doing?" Mama yelled from her own bedroom, in the back of the house.

"She's in my room!"

"I'm in the kitchen!" I yelled. Izzie's room was next to the kitchen. You had to walk through her room to get there. It didn't afford her much privacy, and it gave me a reason to come bother her.

Mama yelled again for me to come out, so I stuck my finger in Izzie's arm one last time and stomped out.

———

Izzie always had her own room and was always kicking me out. When I was little little, if I had a nightmare, I'd sneak into her bed, which meant my brother would wake up and come get in the bed with both of us. She'd get so annoyed, she'd sit up all night, stewing in her irritation until she calmed down and could put us back in our own beds or wake Mama up to do so.

On Saturday mornings, I'd sit on the edge of my sister's bed and we'd watch old kung fu movies. We'd laugh until we cried at the characters who took five minutes to die because they were monologuing with unnaturally bright-red blood seeping from their mouths.

Izzie's room was covered in teen magazine pages and posters of every hot British group of the 1980s. If it was new wave, gothic punk, or any kind of pop alternative music, it was represented on her wall: Duran Duran, Gene Loves Jezebel, Siouxsie and the Banshees, the Cure, the Smiths, the Human League, Bow Wow Wow, Missing Persons, Boy George, George Michael . . . My sister's room was a shrine to MTV. My father said she was weird to like all those "sissy white boys," but he never borrowed her cassettes like he did mine, without returning them. Papering her walls in white singers with their fashionably tacky makeup kept my parents from lingering.

If her TV wasn't on, then she was listening to music. I liked the stuff she listened to, mostly because she liked it, but Duran Duran was my favorite. Her favorite, too. I was singing along to one song for her, acting it out with all my heart, and I turned my head so quickly my glasses flew off my face. I can still see her expression appearing in slow motion as she realized what was happening. Her face went from "Oh no" to shocked amusement, and we both cried laughing at my silliness. We still crack up about it.

My sister would sit at her vanity and put makeup on, the naked lightbulb in her lamp making me squint as I watched her. I asked a million questions: What was that? Why did she make that face to put that on? Why that color? She sighed through her explanations, but she let me stay. She went to three proms, and I watched her get ready each time, wondering if I'd ever be as pretty as she was. She had a gorgeous smile and dimples and smooth dark-brown skin. She knew how to style her own hair, and she could sing. She had pretty handwriting, almost exactly like Mama's, and could draw a little bit. She performed in plays, even landing the role of Maria in *The Sound of Music*. She had talent she could show easily, talent people understood.

I hated her high school boyfriend. When he was over, I couldn't go in her room and dance silly or wiggle my butt at her. I couldn't tease her for watching herself in the mirror or blasting sad white-boy songs. When he was over, I had to be on the lookout, instead of reading my book, and had to hear her clearly exaggerated love noises. She never told *him* to get out of her room.

———

Izzie's husband died in his sleep. She woke up to the alarm on his sleep apnea machine going off. He was the love of her life, a former football player turned preacher from Detroit. They met on the bus. One day, I was answering his first call in the kitchen and telling him she wasn't there as she hid in the hallway; then I blinked, and I was standing next to her in a red bridesmaid's dress as she told him "I do."

When I came home for the funeral, I went to check her mail and saw that someone had stuffed a bag of dinner rolls into the mailbox. We had a good laugh at the well-intended deeds of those hoping to help the grieving. It felt good to make her smile. I felt useless otherwise. Izzie is the nice one between the two of us. She loves people and says hi to strangers, so even in her grief, she was consoling those around her. Oh, I helped with my nephew and did what I could when it came to running errands. The administrative tasks were easy. I can do acts of service with my eyes closed, but I had no idea how to be emotional support. We'd experienced death as a family before, but we all siloed off in our grief, kept our faces averted so no one could see, no one could try to help. What can anyone say to soothe the misery of losing a loved one so unexpectedly? So I picked my nephew up from school and cooked and tried my best to make Izzie laugh, because that's how I love, through action and laughter, and I wanted to make sure she had love on all sides of her.

After her husband died, she got rid of that mattress and moved her bed. Now his side of the bed always has clothes on it, or towels that need to be folded. When I visit her, I skip the den, the usual gathering place in her house, and I go to her room and touch all her lotions and DVDs until I annoy her so much she tells me to get out, just like when we were kids. But I never leave. Wherever my sister finds solace, I will find a way to be there, too.

Prince's Girl

Late at night, WVOL The Mighty 1470 AM would play alternative Black music, like house, electronica, underground hip-hop, the music 92Q FM couldn't or wouldn't play to interrupt its mainstream soul and R&B flavor. We kept the big, fancy stereo system in the living room. The kind with the glass door you had to press softly in one corner to open. It had a turntable, a radio, two cassette decks, and eventually a five-disc CD player, with two speakers on either side of the console that were as tall as I was. Some nights, around 11 p.m. or as late as 1 a.m., I'd push a blank cassette into one of the decks and lightly place my index and middle fingers on the RECORD and PLAY buttons. You had to press them both at the same time in order to record anything. I'd sit there, cross-legged, my head leaning against the left speaker, waiting for the WVOL DJ—sometimes a college student, other times a man with the smirk of wisdom to his voice—to play certain Prince songs.

One night, around the time I was eleven or twelve, I finally got as clean a recording as I could manage of "Girl," at the time the nastiest, sexiest song I'd ever heard in my life.

I don't remember any specific thing that led me to masturbation. It was probably just basic child curiosity about my body. If I hiked my pants up too high, being silly, and the inner seam hit my "cootie-coo" in a weird way, something tumbled through my belly. When I'd lie in bed and stretch, pressing my thighs together so that they pushed against each side of my crotch, something shimmered behind my ear. By the time I heard "Girl," I was taking baths by myself and adjusting the faucet so the water would drip-drip-drip at the rhythm I needed. And I'd been reading enough romance novels to build a pretty good vocabulary of euphemisms for all the sexual body parts.

The first night I heard the song, I was lying on the living room floor, well past my bedtime, reading a book, when Prince's voice breathed over a slurring keyboard for me to "caress the flower." I gasped and sat up. I lowered the volume and pressed my ear against the speaker. No one else in the house could hear this. He said, "Be poetic." My young poet heart stopped. My body turned into a tense, trembling mass of gasps and whimpers, like I'd been overwhelmed by raw power, the electric sea from the song moving through me. Then he said he wanted to be the water in my bath... He wanted to be a wet body lapping against me, surrounding me, being the thing that drip-drip-drips until

I'm carried away into that sea of electricity. I needed this song in my life.

I knew he wasn't talking specifically to me, but how did he know me? Was this what a fully adult sexual relationship was like, this degree of *knowing*?

After that night, I damn near camped out in the living room, waiting to catch the opening notes so I could record it. Sometimes the DJ would talk too far into the song for my liking, or cut it off too early. When I finally got the cleanest recording I could get, I turned everything off and crawled into bed. Until I was fifteen, my brother and I shared a bedroom, so any personal exploration was always in the dead of night when I knew he was deep asleep. I put the tape in my Walkman and slid under my covers. I lay on my back and pulled the pillow over my face. I rewound the tape and pressed PLAY, then pushed the headphones as close to my ears as possible. I had the volume at a good place but didn't want it to be so loud that my brother, or my mother on a late-night bathroom run, would hear.

I got under the covers with Prince's "Girl," but not in the way you might expect. It wasn't a deposit in my spank bank. I was studying this song. I was hearing myself in the lyrics. It was already clear that my fascination with sex was considered inappropriate and uncomfortable. No one in my church had ever explicitly told me sex was a sin, at least not that I could recall, but it was clear to me. The condemnation for being a sexual person hung in the air, shimmying over everything like pollen. And here was Prince, expressing that he, too, sometimes felt bad for the desires he couldn't seem to control. He was only four years younger than my parents, a stranger I knew I'd never meet, but he knew me.

He knew me.

With the pillow over my face, the comforter covering the pillow, I'd made my own little sensory deprivation tank. I wanted nothing to distract me from the song thumping in my ears. It's a sparse track, plinky keyboards and backward vocals sliding in and out of Prince's imploring voice. When he asked if Girl ever gets lonely sometimes, hot tears betrayed me and slid into the curves of my ears. Middle-child syndrome—fully activated. Stuck in between a significantly older sister and a baby brother with "special needs," I often felt lost. I couldn't join my sister and her friends for the grown-up things they did, and my brother couldn't have the kinds of conversations I would've loved to have with him. My mother didn't really care for the friends I had at school at the time, so I didn't do a lot of sleepovers. Instead, I turned to books, music, and television. I entertained myself, but it did get lonely, especially at that preadolescent phase when I started to want boys to notice me. Notice me first, not as an afterthought of my friends. I wanted someone I could talk to. And if we could kiss, that would be even better.

I was around six years old when I first realized who Prince was and those first few years, I was fascinated by this man who looked unlike anyone I had ever seen before. All the future great loves of my life would have some kind of Prince feature: big, pretty eyes; a distinctive mole; a slim, short stature. But as I began to recognize the heat in my blood, I recognized that same heat in his music. I saw myself in this man who seemingly struggled to balance a love for God with his need to be freaky and his need to challenge the way Society with a capital S tells us how we should behave and look as men and women.

I knew Prince was "nasty," but it drew me to him even more. Prince built a reputation on his risqué songs—like "Head," with lyrics about oral sex from a stranger before getting married. It's easy to think that Prince saw women only as objects made for sexual pleasure, but looking deeper, his songs show women with the same sexual urges as men. Although acts like Salt-N-Pepa and Madonna were arguably more important in showcasing women's desires through song at the time, Prince's work resonated more with me.

His '80s catalog, in particular, was a revelatory mix of sex, politics, and religion. He sang as a man unafraid of changing how society looked at masculinity, as a man who enjoyed a more sexually experienced woman, and as a man willing to follow a woman's lead. "Darling Nikki," from the 1984 *Purple Rain* soundtrack, details a one-night stand. It has all the markers to offend—a sex fiend of a woman, masturbating in public, who abandons her conquest after using him. In the sultry song, the object of the woman's affection has no problems with being used and ends the song begging for her to come back.

"If I Was Your Girlfriend," from the 1987 album *Sign o' the Times*, is a song so important to me that I have a line of its lyrics tattooed around my left ankle. In it, Prince's alter ego Camille sings from the perspective of a man who wonders if becoming a woman would lead to a closer relationship with his current female lover. Again, Prince disrupts heteronormative ideals of masculinity in his willingness to change genders for a more significant connection, the kind shared between women. Some people may see this as extreme, maybe even creepy, but it remains to me a fairy-tale example of forever love.

When I started taking Prince's "Girl" to bed with me, it wasn't to get my rocks off. It was to hear a song telling me that someone out there loves and lusts after someone like me. He admits his desire for this person is like a sin and that he can come just from the thought of them. Even in my young mind, I knew that was the ultimate power.

After Prince trails off his sweet talk, there's a collection of licking sounds and gasps on top of some backmasking, which is really Wendy Melvoin, a key member of the Revolution, repeating the lyrics, but with "Boy" instead. The erotic combination thrilled me, my tween mind registering it as what sex is supposed to sound like, not the excessive moans and yells from my father's porn tapes.

By the time I started having sex, I, like most of my peer group, I imagine, would play music in the background. It could help set the mood or cover any sounds in situations with thin walls and nosy roommates. But when I got into my thirties, I realized I no longer wanted to listen to music during sex. It was distracting. I wanted to hear all the slippery sounds and shaky sighs...just like the ending of "Girl."

White Boys

In high school, I had a good guy friend who was white. Bradley seemed to date only Black girls, but no one freaked out about it because he wasn't pretending to be anything other than what he was. He was the cool white guy in a group of Black friends, but not like Vanilla Ice or the lead singer from Color Me Badd. He didn't speak with a "blaccent." He didn't use slang that wasn't a part of his culture. He didn't cut lines into his hair, try to build a high-top fade with hairspray, or invent a background for himself in order to earn points from us Black kids. He wore baseball caps with broken brims and ate microwavable popcorn for dinner. He was just a regular white guy who happened to date Black girls. No big deal.

Some people assumed we hooked up, but we never did. I can't remember how we grew to be friends. It was probably because he was white and kind of quiet. I thought he'd be safe, that my high school boyfriend, Rocco, wouldn't mind my being friends with a white guy. Okay, okay. Bradley and I shared a weird kiss once, during our senior year, after I had broken up with Rocco, but it was a peck, barely any lip flesh involved, both of us trying to figure out if we could be more than friends. We were cuddled on my couch, and I put my arms around him. I moved my hands under his shirt and felt his stomach and back. I remember how soft and doughy his skin felt, and childish me, I assumed that's how all white men felt. All is one, and one is all.

One time, we went through the Taco Bell drive-thru. He was driving. When we got to the window, the guy giving us our order was rude to us for no apparent reason. I asked Bradley about it, if he often received rude looks or slick remarks when he was out with his Black girlfriend. He said it was something he'd had to get used to. It wasn't something I thought I could deal with. Maybe I wasn't ready to date outside of my race. We were barely eighteen at the time, and I was ready to dismiss a wide range of dating experiences by looking outside my race simply because I didn't want to face strangers' rudeness.

After high school graduation, Bradley and I both went to New Orleans for college at different universities. There, I met and fell in love with DJ (who really was a DJ). He came with the typical crew of musician friends—talented men waiting to ride into studio heaven with whoever could get the Big Deal first. When he and I split up, I lashed out by briefly dating the white guy in his crew. (There's always at least one.)

This white guy was much more like Eminem. He used Black vernacular and had a lot of Black friends, but he didn't try to lie about his past for "street cred." Even his rap name was inspired by candy, so he changed it when Eminem seemed to take over hip-hop for a while. My experience with this faux Eminem was not pleasant. I was with him for all the wrong reasons. I knew he'd had a crush on me the entire time I was with DJ, and he was a quick and easy way to hurt my ex.

Once, when stopping by his grandmother's house, Faux Eminem asked me to scrunch down in the passenger seat so no one in the neighborhood would see him with a Black person and report back to her. I was disgusted with him and his cowardice. When he went inside, I leaned my head back against the seat, trying to calm down. I was angry with him and myself. This is one of the reasons why I never really thought I'd date a white guy. I didn't want to hide myself or wonder if I was just a phase or a rebellion. I bounced my knee up and down, a sure sign of anxiety. I halfway wished someone would come up to the car and ask what I was doing, because I wanted to go off. Being with Faux Eminem was mistake enough and now I had to deal with racist bullshit on top of it all. When he came back to the car, I gave him the silent treatment. He apologized and later showed me a poem he'd written about me. The next time he stopped by his grandmother's, she wasn't there, and we went inside for a quickie. I made sure to rub my damp crotch all over the arms of her furniture. I hoped that whenever she napped on her sofa, she dreamed of Black women with big butts parading naked through her home.

When I ended things with Faux Eminem, it was dramatic enough to frighten me a little. He started crying and accused me of lying to him. Faux Eminem was tall, maybe six three, and he loomed over me, demanding I answer his questions. When I fell silent, he broke a VHS tape against the foot of my bed, then slid down the wall into a ball. I watched him, trying to figure out if I would have to call the police. I'd done my best to avoid domestic violence in my personal relationships, and all I could think was, *This is it. This will be the man to punch me, because he's having a tantrum over a breakup.* Thankfully, nothing like that happened. After he was gone, I wondered if his little soap opera scene was part of my penance for using him. And the sex hadn't even been good.

At one point, I had to act like I didn't like head, which I absolutely love, because it was becoming increasingly difficult for me to fake it. And I didn't want to take the time to teach. He started to beg to do it: "C'mon. Let me give you a treat." Offering it to me like it was a dog bone did nothing to make it more appealing. So once again, I found myself deciding I'd never date another white man. Their skin was like Play-Doh; they were too dramatic; and the sex didn't make up for any of it.

———

Time rolled along. After three semi- to quite serious relationships and a few two-month stands, I found myself in grad school again, nursing yet another heartbreak. I was in Los Angeles, overweight, and making less money than I had when I first started working at age sixteen. I felt miserable and unlovable. In LA, I was invisible except to the men who hung out on corners all day and night, and after a while, I welcomed that invisibility. I didn't want anyone to see me anymore. Maybe if I stayed still, I'd disappear completely, and no one else would ever have to think of another excuse to explain why they'd rejected me—my work, my love, my body.

Jeremy saw me on a day I didn't stay still. I was leaving campus, on my way to the bus stop, and he walked up next to me. He carried one of those long skateboards and had dark-brown hair with hazel eyes that changed colors depending on what he wore. They were light brown on the day we met. I don't normally respond to men trying to pick me up on the street, but I felt safe because he was white. When he approached me, it seemed like he was trying to have an actual conversation. He looked me in the eyes. He maintained a respectable distance that didn't crowd me. Then he joked about giving me a ride on his skateboard.

And I know. I keep describing white men as "safe." It's not that they're safer physically than anyone else, but I figured there was no way I could take a white boy's interest in me seriously. I didn't think Jeremy was feeling me like that. White people are nosy, I thought—they'll talk to anyone, just because they can. And even if Jeremy was interested in me, how could anything ever come from it? He had a fit body, and I...did not. Jeremy wanted to get to know me, to be sweet to me, and I wish I had let him, but talking to him, going out with him, magnified all of my insecurities. He had dated Black women before, but based on the way he described them, they were the kind of Black women who would work at Abercrombie & Fitch or American Apparel: slim, fair-skinned, with long, bouncy hair, to hint at the right kind of mixed-race background. I am undeniably Black with a deep-brown complexion. I was fat, with a head full of spirals that would probably never reach past my shoulders. I couldn't even afford American Apparel, let alone try to fit into their clothes or get a job there. It was no fault of his, but being with Jeremy made me shrink more inside myself.

Our first date was lovely. We went to a bookstore, then dinner and a movie. Any man who appreciates a good bookstore date is halfway to being a keeper. On our second date, we went to the beach, and I watched him play volleyball with his friends. I'd brought my camera and was taking pictures of them as they milled around.

"So are you taking pictures for a story? Like for a blog or something?" one of his friends asked. This guy was about six feet tall, with close-cropped dirty-blond sun-streaked hair and the wide shoulders and long arms of a professional swimmer.

"Dude. Nichole's here with me. We're hanging out today," Jeremy replied, and ran his hand up the back of my neck in a clear sign of intimacy. Swimmer Dude's eyes widened in shock as he chirped out, "Cool!" And that pretty much sealed it for me. I wasn't ready. I just couldn't figure out what Jeremy could possibly see in me, someone clearly so different from the other women he'd dated.

We had a cold picnic after his volleyball game. He had

changed shirts in front of me, and the sight of his flat stomach made my body twitch involuntarily. He looked at my face and knew I was trying not to drool, so he smirked at me. I wanted to touch him, to make sure he'd cleaned all the sand from his chest, but then I'd think about my body. I didn't want to see myself naked; how could I let anyone else see me? Especially someone used to thin women, especially someone so fit.

When he took me home, I was quiet, fighting tears. What was my problem? Here was a good guy who took me to bookstores and beaches, who wanted to spend time with me, and I couldn't stop thinking about how awful I was. When he pulled up to my building, I told him.

"Jeremy, I had a really good time today, but I don't think I can see you again." I kept my hand on the door so I could open it quickly.

"Is this about Swimmer Dude? I'm really sorry about that, and I chewed him out right before we started playing. He's just a dick." He turned his body to me and pulled my hands into his.

"No, it's not about him. Well, not really. I mean…" I sighed, and he shook our hands lightly, as if reminding me he was still holding on. I forced myself to look in his eyes, even though mine felt prickly, and I blurted it all out.

"I just don't think I'm ready to see anyone. I've got too many issues, and it doesn't seem like I'm the type of woman you'd be interested in. I thought I'd be okay with that, but I'm not. And it's not really you. It's me. Which sounds crappy, and I'm sorry. But look at us. Look at me!"

"You're beautiful!" Jeremy said. "I don't understand what you're talking about." He leaned forward and moved his hands to my wrists. He had nice, warm hands. They felt a little grubby after the beach, but he held my wrists loosely so I'd know I could break free any time I wanted.

"Why would I not want to be with you? You're not making sense. Is it an ex?" Jeremy tried his best to understand, but I was too broken. I could never trust his affection because I couldn't see myself as worthy of it. He could keep telling me how beautiful I was, that he loved making me laugh, but it wouldn't be enough.

For a long time, I kicked my own ass over how I handled him. Maybe I should've let him love me into loving myself, like in the movies, but I had already used one white boy. I didn't want to use another one to pull myself out of the mire of depression and low self-esteem. I frequently wondered if I had done the right thing by Jeremy, and I promised myself that if I ever had another opportunity to date a white guy, I'd give it a proper chance.

———

Two years after leaving grad school again and moving back home, I asked friends to meet me at a comedy club for my birthday. At this point, I had stopped hiding and was hoping I could meet the world halfway. At the table behind us, there was a white guy you'd overlook in a crowd. He was about five ten, with a compact, tight little body, a crew cut of dark-brown hair, and glasses. He was so plain he could've been either a mouse or a serial killer, but something about him set off my Good Lover Radar™. I mentioned him to my friend Lee, and she went over and somehow got us to introduce ourselves to each other. It was very much like high school, but I was drunk—and excited about setting my white-boy karma record straight.

Devon and I exchanged texts and spoke on the phone for hours. We met for lunch, then planned our first big date—a night at a local film festival. While we were standing in line, a woman at another booth gestured Devon over and gave him free tickets. Once we had our seats inside the theater, Devon went to get snacks and came back with free drinks. Twice in one night, someone had given him free shit.

"Do you know any of those people?" I asked, a little bewildered.

"Nah," he said. "I guess they were just being nice."

Struck that his white male privilege had benefited us both that night, I settled in to watch a collection of short films, feeling stunned yet smug. This was probably the only time I wasn't resentful of white men getting stuff handed to them for no reason. One of the reasons I typically stayed away from white men is because they often pretended to be obtuse about how their whiteness and maleness helped them get ahead in life. They get offended when you bring up their race, because they bring up race only in negative contexts, so they assume everyone else does, too. Who would want to have to convince someone they're intimate with about racial disparities and privilege? It's too exhausting.

After dinner, we went to a fancy hotel in downtown Nashville. As we walked past displays of country music singers' guitars, boots, and outfits, I started to get nervous. We had planned the hotel stay, so I wasn't surprised, but I had started thinking about my body. Would it be too much, too Black for him? I don't wear perfume often, preferring to wear scented lotions and oils. In the hotel bathroom, I freshened up and wondered if I smelled too fruity, like a teenager high on Bath & Body Works. I was too old to smell like glitter fruit. Would he even be able to get it up?

Back in the bedroom, I confessed how nervous I was. He tried to kiss me, but I couldn't get into it. His thin lips made me think of Angela Lansbury as Jessica Fletcher in *Murder, She Wrote*. Would I ever solve the mystery of what the hell I was doing with my life that had led me here? I turned my head to hide the image, and Devon did good work on my neck before easing down, down, down. When he finally made it to Lady Marmalade and got in one good lick, I gasped, "Oh, what the fuck!"

I have been blessed with some very skilled and gifted lovers, and my Good Lover Radar™ is about 90 percent accurate. Part of my healthy appreciation for sex is because of how pleasurable it's been for me most of the time. And when I say this white boy did something to me that made me question what kind of head I'd received prior, I want my praise for him and his skill set to be clear. After my initial shock, my mind went blank. Then the writer in me crawled through the blankets of bliss, and I tried to pay attention so I could be precise when I told my girlfriends what he did.

The overall sex was good, too. Average penis, solid rhythm. He did what I needed him to do, and we had about two or three rounds before falling asleep. In the morning, I was hoping for more, but he made it pretty clear that he had to get back to his dog, and the shine wore off. As I rolled my body out of bed, I rolled my eyes as well. White people and dogs, man.

We tried to make arrangements for another date, but it became clear that he was dodging. The mojo that had been hibernating inside me for the last few years had woken up fully and completely. It had pushed back the curtains and blasted me full of sun. How dare he not want more of this? What was wrong with him? I was angry. My mojo was pacing a hole in my mind. Maybe I had been terrible. Maybe the years of inconsistent sex and depression had killed my sexuality.

Devon is the only guy I've ever had sex with who didn't make a concerted effort for more, and it fucked with me. Boyfriends from high school, men who haven't seen me naked in almost twenty years, still tried to get in my pants. And I barely knew what I was doing back then! So why was this one dude tripping? Why couldn't I make anything work with white men? Not that my record with Black men was stellar...

I became obsessed with dating a white man, and not because I thought a white man would save me from spinsterhood or because I thought Black men were terrible. It was because if I could overcome the challenges presented in an interracial relationship, I could conquer all of my relationship issues. Right?

———

I tried to date the old-fashioned way. I made an effort to go out more, but I still wasn't having much luck. Finally, I decided to try online dating, just to get my feet wet. I'd done the Match.com and eHarmony thing before, but it never felt right. Now there were apps like Tinder and OkCupid, where matching with someone felt more like a game. The Black men sent me messages that were clearly their "Sunday best." They told me how they needed a queen and were looking to get married. They marveled at how someone as pretty as me could even need a dating app. They sent immediate pleas to meet up and lick my toes and/or ass. The white men asked if I would dominate them or let them dominate me. Some white guys offered to suck dick to prove their worthiness to me. And almost all of them, regardless of race or ethnicity, failed miserably at spelling.

I wasn't fooling myself that I'd find the love of my life on OkCupid, but I had a few dates with a collection of white guys. There was the older man who looked like a photograph of Dudley Moore that someone had licked. When he reached out to me, it was with that old gambit "Hey, I'm in town for business and would love for you to be my tour guide." I went back and forth on how to respond to him, but finally I said, "Fuck it," and gave him a list of demands. I wanted to be worshipped. I did not want to reciprocate. He eagerly agreed. I made sure my friends knew where I would be, then met him for drinks downtown.

We had a surprisingly solid connection. Our conversation flowed. We talked about movies, television, and literature.

We shared opinions about the best places to live and visit in the country, and we were able to make each other laugh. It takes a lot to get me comfortable enough to have a smooth conversation. In the hotel room, the topics became sexual, of course. I gave him my list of limits, and he asked clarifying questions. He was respectful and accommodating. I felt very lucky that I didn't end up with a racist sex murderer.

We got down to business...Well, after my weekend with Freaky Todd, the name I used when I talked about him to my girlfriends, I started to believe that white men's true superpower is their ability to give head. Are reparations in white boys' mouths? I wouldn't say yes, but I wouldn't say no either.

At one point in the night, I was limp, warm tears of praise leaking quietly from the corners of my eyes. He had a huge dick and lightly complained that I was too tight. It had been a while, but I'd been with men who had larger dicks and they'd never complained about snugness. In fact, they seemed to love it. Regardless, Freaky Todd seemed to think my fit was a result of nervousness or anxiety so he went down to get me to relax, and I felt no reason to stop him.

Freaky Todd tried to get me to stay over every night of his stay, but I always refused. He was a cuddler, and after his orgasms, he would wrap around me like we were reenacting the Lennon-Ono *Rolling Stone* cover, his knee raised over my belly, arm curving across my chest. He constantly trailed his fingers along my skin and complimented my softness. He even got me to confess my most secret sexual fantasy. (No, I'm not sharing it here.) When I told him, he laughed, pulled me in close, kissed my cheek, and called me a delight. He said he hoped I'd find someone who would bless me with that fantasy, because I deserve pleasure in everything. I felt genuinely moved. I wasn't expecting something that was so clearly and explicitly a hookup to be so intimate.

Then there was a former traffic reporter for a radio station. He was tall and slim, but he was also cheap. His sex talk sounded like he was still on the air. His voice was booming yet soothing, with oddly accented enthusiasm. I didn't think people actually said "Oh yeah, baby" during sex in real life, but he did. He frequently mentioned his white dick during sex. If I hadn't already told him I hated the word "cock," he would have been a porn parody. Whenever he would say something like "Look at my *white* dick in *your* hands, baby," I had the impression that something about my Black pussy would be next, and that kind of talk is not allowed in my proverbial bedroom. He'd bring up his whiteness, and I'd go still and quiet, so he eventually got the hint and shut up. I ended that over text shortly after we became physically intimate: "We don't seem compatible, but thanks for trying."

———

Ultimately, white men are still men. Fresh haircut confidence is universal. They all take food into the bathroom because they're gross. They all think they deserve a model with a doctorate in a STEM subject who's also a chef and painter, who can deep-throat, and who won't ask them to explain why they've disappeared for a week. But every now and then, there's someone who saves you the last bit of chocolate ice cream from a container of Neapolitan or who buys you books of poetry, and it doesn't matter that he's white. Yes, I have to bring my own washcloths or constantly repeat that I don't want anal sex, but I do deserve pleasure in all things, and if that comes with blue eyes and a high tolerance for mayonnaise and cold weather, then so be it.

It makes a cruel kind of sense that the next time I fell in love, it was (1) with a white guy and (2) with someone I could never tell I loved him: The Russian. He was my favorite. We went on hikes and to the opera. He cooked for me. When he wanted to get frisky, he'd say, "Come sit next to me." If I wanted to leave before he wanted me to, he'd say, "Well, have something to eat first," and I'd end up spending the night again. He had red hair, muscular, pretty thighs, and strong, wide hands. He constantly played new music for me and made me drink kefir when I was constipated and growled when we made out and bought me Cara Cara oranges and emailed me GIFs that featured Keanu Reeves, because he knew how much I loved that monotone fool, and watched *Frasier* like I watch *Frasier*—over and over yet like it was the first time—and once spent an hour breaking my car free of ice and snow. He was newly divorced and never wanted to get married again or even have another serious relationship, so when I fell for him, I tucked my love in chess pies and greens and trinkets from Etsy and kisses against his forehead.

He was a darling man, but I listened to what he said and

not what he did, so I never told him with words how I felt about him. The Russian was also a smart and observant man, so I'm sure he knew. When our untitled relationship began to make him feel something he didn't want to feel again, he was kind in his leaving but gone all the same.

The unspoken love I felt for this man refreshed me. And it scared me. It had taken so long to get to him, to have a balanced exchange of affection, trust, and respect. The fact that he was white added an extra layer to our discussions about current events, to be sure. Yes, he definitely said things that bordered on offensive, and I'd have to check him, but then he'd make me soup from scratch when I was sick. He'd Skype me from across town when he was drunk and feeling silly. I would complain of being cold, and he'd place his warm hands on my back. Those things had nothing to do with race and everything to do with a generous and thoughtful kindness we should all be so lucky to experience.

I don't know if dating all these white boys has helped me become a better partner, but falling for The Russian helped me stop worrying about the what-ifs. What if I can't escape this pattern of attracting men who don't want anything long-term, at least not with me, or what if there is no one after him? Well. Yes. That's the thing, isn't it? Regardless of the duration, there will be no one else who cares for me in the same way, so I learned to stand firmly in the singularity of love, unspoken yet clear and worth every moment it took to arrive.

Janet Jackson and the
All-Black Uniform

My parents liked to send messages to each other via song. The entire song didn't necessarily have to apply to whatever situation was going on in their marriage. The chorus was the most important part, even just a line or two. My father would come home after being God knows where when he should've been at work, and my mother would cue up "It's Over Now" by Luther Vandross. It was a song about someone suspicious that his lover was cheating. The chorus went: "You did me bad / It's over now / You treated me so bad / It's over now…" I don't know if my mother really thought he was cheating. I just think she wanted to let him know she knew he had not been doing what he should have, and she was over it.

Depending on my father's mood, he'd give as good as he got, usually with Rick James's "Cold Blooded." The song was about how sexy Rick's lover was and how he hoped she'd return his attention, but my father focused on that repeated chorus of "She's cold...blooded." He wanted to call her cold because she couldn't tolerate the way he'd neglect his responsibilities. I got to hear a lot of good music because of my parents' coded fighting.

In 1986, Janet Jackson's album *Control* began to take the world by storm, and the eponymous single rocked my home. My mother's passive-aggressive game skyrocketed. Janet was twenty and ready to establish herself as more than Michael's little sister. She wanted to show the world her independence, talent, and maturity. My mother was thirty-two. She'd never lived alone. A teenage mother, she went from her childhood home, following the rules of the grandmother who raised her, into what would become an abusive marriage, and she'd never had a chance to establish her own identity. Although Janet was much younger with a vastly different childhood, I think my mother connected to Janet's journey of finding and asserting herself. And Mama was losing patience with my father, his addictions, his abuse, his irresponsibility. She had been working as a nurse at the same clinic since before I was born. In every corner of her life, she was taking care of someone— her patients, her children, and her trifling-ass husband. Mama was tired and ready to gain control over her life.

Enter Janet Jackson's third album and its lead single.

If my mother started playing "Control," it was for a few reasons:

1. It annoyed my father.
2. She was giving herself a musical pep talk.

3. She was letting my father know that for all his abusive bluster, she was the decision maker in the household.
4. The album was banging, and no one could deny that.

When *Control* came out, MTV and BET played music videos around the clock. Janet released a video with every single. She danced her heart out, creating choreography that's been passed all the way down to the TikTok generation. In most of the videos from this album, Janet wears all-black attire. I was eight years old at the time and didn't think much about it until I overheard someone say that black was slimming and that Janet was trying to hide her chubbiness.

———

I don't know when my body image issues began, but they feel as part of me as my moles. When I was a little girl, I was so skinny and small people always thought I was younger than I was. As a tween, my worst fear was that someone would say I looked like a boy. All those fast-developing friends magnified my lack of curves. I'd stand in front of the mirror, wondering when my hips and breasts would arrive. My mother laughed at me and told me I wouldn't want them when I got them, but I was impatient and envious.

A late bloomer, I envied Janet's all-black uniform and how it was supposed to hide her shape from the world. I wanted that. I needed to hide. I didn't have the shape a Black girl was supposed to have, so I wanted to make myself invisible.

Wearing fashionable, pretty clothes with bright colors and interesting patterns got compliments, but it also had people looking at your body. I didn't want to bring any more attention to my lack of breasts or whatever else I thought was the marker of moving into womanhood. So when junior high hit, and my parents finally divorced, about three years after *Control* came out, I started adding more and more black clothing to my wardrobe.

Mama hated it. She loved to stand out—with animal prints and colorful earrings. She wore slips with denim skirts. She dressed in a way that let everyone know she was both woman and lady. My sister was her girly girl, but I hated the pinks and flower prints my mom tried to dress me in. I wanted plain T-shirts and black jeans and black sweatshirts and black dresses. All I could think about was "Black is slimming," so if I had nothing to begin with, maybe in all black I could totally disappear.

———

As my parents' relationship withered, Janet's career as an independent woman and artist grew. Her waistline shrank. Her clothes became more colorful and covered less flesh. My body changed, too. I got hips and a little bit of boobs and a healthy portion of ass, but I still wanted to hide. The ass brought too much attention. I understood why. It was the perfect shape to welcome faces. (It still is; there's just a bit more of it now.) Guys I dated wanted me to show off—but not too much.

I remember my college boyfriend and me leaving a friend's house where ten or so dudes were "making music" (read: smoking weed and playing video games) and he scanned the room to make sure no one was watching my ass in the tank dress I was wearing. I can't front. It had a really nice jiggle back then.

The thing is, I gained the college freshman 15 and then the sophomore 10 and the junior 10. My curves filled out, and I had the perfect southern-woman silhouette...and still I wanted to hide.

Yes, I'd been waiting for my Coke-bottle shape since I was eight years old, but I was supposed to have a flat belly and overflowing breasts, too. Instead, the curves came with a little belly that I had to suck in and breasts that were still small (but perky) as hell.

My mother would look at me and my new filled-out shape and become emotional. "You're such a woman now," she'd say before commenting on my big legs. Then she'd launch into a series of memories about how little I used to be.

I'd been getting harassed on the street since I was seven years old, so I learned very early on that men will say anything to see how far they can go. That a compliment becomes a threat as soon as you ignore a man. Now, men watched me with even more attention.

Everyone had such different reactions to my changing, late-blooming body, that I kept pulling out my Janet Jackson uniform, kept trying to disappear again into the mystery of all black.

When I was twenty-five, I finally fell in love with my body. I was working out semiregularly. I was exploring casual sex and not worrying about whether men found me marry-able. I loved the power I felt in my body, and then it betrayed me. My spleen spontaneously ruptured, and I had to have emergency surgeries that left me with IBS (irritable bowel syndrome). The PCOS (polycystic ovary syndrome) that had gone undiagnosed since my teenage years began causing me problems, like weight gain, increasingly irregular periods, and other digestive issues. The significant scar from my surgeries sliced my torso in half, from just under my breasts to the top of my pubic area. It moved through my belly button, leaving it crooked and no longer a place for a lover's tongue. Instead, it left me self-conscious about my body and my wardrobe again. I could no longer wear the crop tops that highlighted my small waist. I had to be careful about bodycon dresses so they wouldn't show the puffiness of my scar or how one side of my belly had healed weirdly and now sticks out farther than the other in a way that sucking in cannot hide.

Whatever color my wardrobe had gained in the brief time I loved my body was pushed to the side to make room for more black.

Black is slimming. Make me disappear.
Black is slimming. Make me disappear.
If you can't see me, you can't see all the ways I'm not perfect.

———

I'm older now and more resigned to accept that whatever shape my body is, that's just its shape. I didn't want to spend so much of my time stressing over my body. I tried for so long to be invisible, but I'm here. It feels like my life is finally starting, and I want my life to be bright and colorful. I still wear a lot of black, but I love reds, corals, yellows, blues, and purples.

During my midthirties, I compromised with myself and began wearing gray, accentuating it with bright colors. Shortly after my forties began, I joined a clothes styling service at a department store, and every two to three months, a professional stylist would suggest outfits for me. I asked him to give me colors and patterns; otherwise, I'd fall back on old habits. I don't know that I'll ever love my body again, but I'm fine with it. My body is a hormonal, shapeless mess, but it's keeping me alive (and this pussy still yanks, so . . . I'm good).

Janet Jackson's *Control* helped empower my mother to eventually break free from a disastrous marriage. Someone's gossipy throwaway comment about Janet's weight and shape sent me on a thirty-year mission of hide-and-seek with my body. That's not Janet's fault. I latched on to this comment to gain control over how my body was viewed, but it never really worked. Everyone saw what they wanted to see, even myself.

Softness

> your skin was always soft
> you stayed moisturized
> you was supple
>   *—Text messages from an ex-boyfriend*

Sometimes I think about Serena Williams. All the many ways she's been called masculine because of the shade of her skin, the strength of her arms, the power of her skills while simultaneously being lusted over because of her curvy figure. She wears tutus when she plays, and her wedding had Disney princess flourishes, but because she grunts or displays a temper when treated unfairly, she gets called a man. Serena is so many things—she has a clothing line, makes jewelry, went to school to learn how to do nails—but her focused athleticism intimidates many, so they resort to the laziest insult. Her treatment reminds me that for people who believe gender exists as a binary, there are only absolutes. You are either masculine or you're feminine, and there's no room for nuance.

In 2004, Maria Sharapova won Wimbledon against Serena. She has since lost to Serena nineteen times, and yet their relationship has been labeled a rivalry. Sharapova got lucrative brand and modeling deals and made it a point to highlight how she didn't want to become too muscular while training, a dig at Serena's build. Despite being six two to Serena's five nine, Sharapova is seen as the dainty one, the feminine one. Perhaps Sharapova's fear of being unattractive is why she could not seem to beat Serena again, why Serena has surpassed her to become one of the greatest tennis players of all time. Sharapova was even suspended for over a year for using a forbidden substance, although she played the innocent victim. It could be said that the need for femininity led her to make career-disrupting decisions, and now she's retired at thirty-three, while Serena, currently thirty-nine, keeps going.

I don't want an outdated idea of femininity to keep me from being my best self.

———

I'm terrible at flirting. I'm too up-front. I don't want to be coy. *Barney voice*: You like me / I like you / Let's go see what it do. I'm not particularly smooth and, in fact, can be pretty awkward, but I believe in putting my cards on the table. I don't want to waste my time. But men like to chase, the world tells me. In my early twenties, my mother and sister would tell me, "Men like to feel like men." I'm not sure how being up-front about what I want or refusing to deal with bullshit means I've changed someone's entire gender, but that's the kind of stuff people would repeat ad nauseum so that I would soften up and become more feminine. However, the woman who bats her lashes and plays dumb to impress a guy has never felt good on me. I've tried that personality several times, and it pinched me to the point of numbness. Banter is great, but I can volley only so many times before I want to throw down my tennis racket and jump the net, you know?

————

When I started kindergarten, Muh'Deah gave me a navy-blue dress with red flowers (or maybe strawberries) all over it. It had cap sleeves and was A-shaped, so it flared out from under my arms and made me look like a little bell, or so I thought. I loved that dress. I was so excited to wear it to school, and my mom loved it, because she's always liked seeing her children dressed up. She's been particular about clothes as long as she's been on this earth. Maybe we didn't always have a lot of money, but my mom made sure we looked good. She loves shopping for clothes, especially stuff that's on sale. She's one of those women who can stick her hands into the messiest clothes rack in a store and pull out the only pretty item marked down to three dollars. Unfortunately, I don't have that gift.

I went to kindergarten feeling like a pretty little bell. I was a little nervous, too, because it was the first day of real school, not day care, but my sister was in the same building so I felt like everything would be okay. While waiting in line in the cafeteria for lunch, I looked around for Izzie. One of the older students walked by me and said out loud, "I thought that little girl was pregnant!" She and some other girls started laughing and looking at me, and all the pleasure of my little bell dress disappeared. I felt self-conscious and embarrassed, even though I didn't know why. I spent the rest of lunchtime trying to hide the shape of my dress by folding it under my legs when I sat.

By the time recess came, I had forgotten about my embarrassment in anticipation of the monkey bars. I loved the playground and swinging as high as I could on the swings. Crossing the monkey bars made me feel like a superhero. I could skip a bar and move so quickly my friends would call me a show-off. Playing outside, I would feel the freedom of the wind against my face as I tried to find the bluest corner of the sky.

I was hanging from one set of bars, waiting for the kids in front of me to move along so I could have my turn to cross. A boy walked up to me and asked if I wanted to be his girlfriend. I said, "No! My mama said we can't have no boyfriends till we in high school." I kicked my feet out a little bit so I could have the momentum I'd need to swing forward, and he grabbed one of my legs to hold me in place and ran his other hand up my leg, trying to get to my underwear. I screamed and kicked with my other leg. I yelled out how nasty he was, and I was able to land a kick or two before he let me go. Then I dropped down from the monkey bars and ran to the picnic table where the teachers sat while pretending to watch us.

"Mrs. S, that boy tried to touch my privacy!" I declared, pointing a shaky finger at him. He had scared me. Nobody was supposed to touch me anywhere my clothes covered, so why did he do that? I could tell my teacher wanted to laugh, and the other women at the table turned their smiles away. I couldn't understand: Why was everyone laughing at me? I just wanted to look pretty in my dress and fly free on the monkey bars. But somehow I had become a joke. It didn't make sense.

By the time I got home, I'd resolved never to wear that dress, or any other dress, to school ever again. Little girls are supposed to wear dresses, but in my mind, it gave people permission to make fun of me and to make me uncomfortable with my own body. That boy had put his hands on me, and even though I'd fought back, I had been worried about how I could control the situation without exposing my panties, because that's another rule: Little girls have to wear dresses, but make sure no one can see your "imagination." (That's country old folks talk for your coochie, as in "Nicki, pull your dress down. I can see your imagination.") Wearing dresses came with too many rules, and even if you did nothing wrong, you could still end up violated somehow. So in my little-girl mind, I vowed: No more dresses at school.

Now, Mama will tell you she still put me in dresses for school, but the way I remember it is fighting and fussing to wear pants and shorts. I'd wear dresses to church, but that was it. One time, my grandfather bought me a floofy pink dress for my birthday, and when I pulled it out of the box I said, in as disgusted a tone as an eight-year-old can manage, "*Another dress?*" Mama pulled me into the kitchen, under the guise of fixing drinks for everyone, and talked to me, so I had to come back out and apologize and tell Gran'daddy I really liked it.

My refusal to wear dresses or let Mama buy me flower-print anything was my own personal rebellion against the patriarchy, even though I hadn't heard of that word yet. When I protested, Mama would try to cajole me: "Don't you want to look pretty? Don't you want to look like a cute little girl?" Meanwhile, I was thinking, *What would I look like in pants? Am I only cute, only a girl in a dress? I'm a girl all the time no matter what I wear!* My sister is the opposite. Izzie played with dolls and collected Barbie stuff while I chewed my Barbie dolls' hands and feet and broke their legs so I could see their "bones." Izzie wore dresses regularly and played in makeup. She enjoyed going to church and sang in the choir. She waved at strangers and always had a nice smile for people. She could talk to anyone, and everyone would tell Mama what a little lady Izzie was. I was not a little lady.

The thing is, I wasn't even a tomboy. Southern folks can excuse a lack of ladylike behavior if you're athletic, good with your hands, or something along those lines. If you're a girl with a masculine presentation, it has to have a purpose that still serves others. If you're an athlete, you can help bring in a school championship. If you can fix cars, you can give people discounts or keep the family car going. And even though it might make them frown up or think nasty thoughts, people can understand if a woman dresses like a boy and likes girls; if you want to look like a man, it makes a certain kind of sense you wanted to "act like a man" in other ways. But if you don't like wearing dresses and you don't act like a tomboy and you're attracted to men but don't dress like you want to attract men, no one knows how to classify you. They just know you're lacking somehow.

No one could figure me out, and because of it, I felt like I didn't belong anywhere. I don't like playing sports. I abandoned track in junior high, because I felt like my time was better occupied by reading. I devoured romance novels but did little else to validate my femininity. How could I like romance novels, the ultimate sign of empty-headed girliness, but not wear dresses or like the color pink? When my classmates started paying attention to the paperbacks in my bookbag, they'd laugh before saying I didn't seem like the type to like "those kinds of books." I showed them the pages where I'd underlined all the sex scenes in red, and that seemed to explain everything. I was a flat-chested, skinny, bucktoothed, four-eyed girl with terrible hairstyles that no boy was really interested in, and yet I turned everything into a discussion about sex. I didn't fit neatly into any box.

When I finally became shapely like a woman and started wearing dresses willingly, I was told that they were the wrong dresses—too short, too tight. And that my red lipstick was inappropriate. I finally looked like a girl but the wrong kind of girl. First, too boyish, and now, too womanly. When would my body ever be right?

Serena Williams has faced similar hypocritical judgments. During the 2018 French Open, she once wore an athletic jumpsuit that covered her entire body, leaving only her face and arms visible, and was scolded for dressing too provocatively. Never mind that she wore the jumpsuit because the compression garment was helping her manage a serious medical condition. People could see her bold curves, and it made them uncomfortable. How could they say she's too masculine while warning her to cover the shape of her breasts and ass? What does it mean that they could possibly be turned on by the body of a woman they swear is unattractive? All of these internal biases projected onto Serena's exterior encroach upon her life and mine. They all send a clear picture: People expect women to be everything at once, and there is no way to please everyone.

I was in New York and freelancing when this unnecessary uproar happened, and it instantly jolted me back to an episode from my previous more traditional work life. I was an administrative assistant and was wearing gray slacks from The Limited and a pink oxford shirt with cuffed sleeves. My department was having a meeting, and I stood to give my report. My booty was in serious poke-out mode, and the slacks emphasized its shape. An older woman, a department head's executive assistant, tutted loudly at me, rolled her eyes, and turned away with a huff. Several people around us noted her actions and widened their eyes. She went red in the face, and I self-consciously pulled at my shirt to make sure it was in place, only to realize that she was simply disgusted by the shape of my ass, annoyed that the body I had was not unremarkable.

———

I knew what I wanted: to hide away from judging eyes, to reject the expectations of what a woman had to look like to be respected, while being soft and naughty and femme underneath it all for me and mine (but mostly for me). As much as

I loved Prince, I could never pull off androgyny like he did, and I didn't want to appear androgynous, but I did draw on his attitude of doing what suited him—fuck everybody else. After years of being assessed and found lacking somehow, I decided I would please myself. I knew I'd never be fashionable enough or shaped right or properly dressed, so I began to pay attention to the parts of me that only those granted intimacy would know. I resented people trying to be the authority on my body. A quick scan, and they think they know you.

Beneath Serena's tennis skirts, she is a Disney princess. Beneath my all-black attire, beneath the T-shirt and jeans, I wear the sheerest, sexiest underwear I can find. I've never really cared for perfume, but I rub scented lotion into my thighs, so that every time I go to the bathroom, I smell the extra sweetness of me and want to kiss my damn self. While my sister played in makeup as a child, I played in my mother's scented lotions. Today, I exfoliate my skin with loofahs to make it as soft as possible. I also use shower gloves and body scrubs. My mother and sister tease me about how greasy I am because I keep my body so well moisturized. I will definitely leave cocoa- and mango-butter handprints on every slick surface. Someone out there will try to tell me I shouldn't do so much to my skin, but please keep that crunchy-skin nonsense to yourself.

In my late thirties, I was diagnosed with some kind of adult-onset eczema due to stress. (I really hated my job at the time.) Not to be too dramatic about it, but I cried. Patches of dry, bruised-looking skin decorated my arms, thighs, and cheeks. My skin, my secret weapon of mass femininity, was betraying me. It was the thing I always answered whenever anyone asked, "What do you like most about your body?" When I'm getting to know someone on a dating app, I like to ask what their favorite compliment is that they've received from an ex. Sometimes they say something sweet but boring like, "I'm good at making them laugh." Sometimes they say what they think I want to hear: "I was the first person to make her come." (Sure, dude.) Whatever they answer, they send the question back to me, and I say, "Well, I'll tell you my second favorite..." I won't tell them my top compliment because I don't want them to regurgitate it. The best thing, my most favorite compliment, is to tell me how soft my skin is, but I want it to be organic. I want to surprise a lover with how much he wants to keep touching me.

It doesn't matter how strict the French Tennis Federation makes its dress code; Serena still wins. Just like it doesn't matter what kind of clothes I wear or how bold my mouth is; I'm still a woman. I've been too skinny and too fat. I don't spend enough on my clothes, and they don't flatter me. I should wear a belt with jeans, even though it irritates me, to make it look like I have a waist, or I should wear a dress—not too short, not too long—so everyone knows I'm a lady. But when you touch me, when you feel the care I put into my skin, all the noise about my appearance fades away. I am something you want to melt into. I am a soft thing. Everyone wants to take care of soft things.

———

There was a guy I hooked up with for about a year that I nick-named The Hippie. The Hippie and I had been seeing each other for a few months, and it had become painfully obvious how difficult it was to get him to compliment me. By this point, I'd discovered the secret to opening him up was liquor. That's how he'd loosen up enough to remember I was a human being who enjoyed occasional praise. One random summer night, I was going over to his place, so I took an extra special get-some shower: That's a regular, thorough shower plus any necessary hair removal, but add a sugar scrub and a sweet-scented moisturizing body wash, then a complementary body butter topped with my uniquely scented body oil. (This oil is top secret, and I always buy multiple bottles at a time, in case the business closes down.) Chill for a minute to let everything absorb, then get dressed. Since it was already pretty late, I threw on a bulky sweatshirt, leggings, and tennis shoes. I didn't even bother with gloss, just a high-sheen lip balm. When I got there, he said, "You look comfortable," and I rolled my eyes. I guess he was expecting me to show up in a teddy or something.

He was already a few beers in and buzzing enough to tell me I smelled good and he liked my hair. When we got upstairs and all my comfortable clothes were on his floor, he rubbed a hand down my back and I heard him inhale sharply. He got behind me and kept running his hands all over my hips, ass, and back, more so than he ever had before. Finally, he lowered his face to my back and whispered, "You are always so soft"— so low I almost didn't hear him. Then he kissed my spine.

Game. Set. Match.

My Brother the Superhero

When My Brother Was Little [2]

He liked to carry sticks.
They had to be a certain length and thickness.
Only he knew the precise length and thickness.
My neighbor watched my brother have a conversation
  with himself
and said how freeing it must be to live in a private world.
Every Sunday I prayed God would make him normal.

When my brother was little,
he loved He-Man, Voltron, Superman, and the Incredible
  Hulk.
He would put together the Voltron lions

---

2   I wrote this poem for my brother in my book *Lilith, but Dark*
     (Publishing Genius, 2018).

and sit the super robot creation in its own chair.
If you moved it, his cries would peel the walls down
around us.
My brother pretended to be He-Man and punched holes
in those walls. He would hide this evidence of strength
behind masking tape that blended perfectly.
He was clever and sneaky like any other boy.

My brother is a grown man now.
He still loves superheroes,
especially the ones that get to break free
of their skin.

For about twenty-five years, Nashville had an amusement park called Opryland USA. It was dedicated to all things Grand Ole Opry and country music. It shut down in 1997 because it wasn't all that easy and tourist-friendly to get to and, because Nashville does indeed get cold and snowy sometimes, it couldn't run in the winter. People didn't want a job that was only March to October, with no guarantee they'd be rehired for the next season, so the employee pool got smaller and smaller, until the park's owners decided to close it for good and build out the mall and hotel that's there now.

Opryland had the usual amusement park stuff: roller coasters and teacup rides, plus concerts. Nashville is Music City USA, after all. I'm not sure how many times I was there as a child with school or church field trips, but it was enough. I am not wild about amusement parks. They are too crowded. They're too noisy. The food is usually terrible. Everything costs too much. It all gives me a headache.

The summer before I headed to college, my church went on a field trip to Opryland. I didn't want to go, but my mother made me so I could be there with my brother. J is into amusement parks and water parks. I think he likes the noise and he gets to watch everyone in the crowds. He loves swimming and all things superhero, especially Superman, Batman, and Spider-Man. J loves R&B, especially Faith Evans. When he finds a favorite riff or a favorite television theme song, he listens to it over and over. He's broken so many cassette and compact disc players over the years because he wears out the PLAY/PAUSE and REWIND buttons. He's the same way with favorite movies. The more action scenes, the louder the crashes, the better. We had to get him headphones so he could listen to his favorite moments on repeat without disturbing the entire household. When tablets became popular, I bought him one for Christmas, and I have to buy him a new one every two years to make sure he has something that still works. He runs through electronics like I go through hairstyles.

So I went to Opryland with our church to make sure J would be okay and get to experience everything he wanted. My nerves were already a mess at the thought of being in the middle of so much chaos, but I was also feeling tender because I'd be leaving for school and I wouldn't be there to protect J anymore.

My mother never allowed us siblings to fight. She firmly

believed brothers and sisters looked out for each other and should not be mean to each other in the home, when the world would bring enough of that to us on the outside. I often hear people talking about the roughhousing they did with their siblings, but we didn't do that. And once it became clear that my brother was going to be "different," my mother made sure I knew I had to keep watch over him. I took my job very seriously. He and I are two years apart, and we went to school together starting in day care. When he was young, he was nonverbal for a long time. I remember once at day care when he came out of the bathroom with his pants and under-wear around his ankles, looking for me and screaming, his eyes running over with tears. The boys had done something to him to humiliate him, and I was the first person he came to for help. He must have been around three years old, which meant that I was five. I immediately pulled his pants up and hugged him, but I don't remember much after that, beyond my yelling at everyone in the room. The day-care workers, probably in an attempt to control the situation and avoid any trouble, simply told my mother, "She looks out for her little brother, I tell you that."

The summer before I left for New Orleans, my brother and I were making the rounds at Opryland when I suggested we get something to eat. It was an odd time of day to eat, I guess, because no one else was in the pizza place we stopped at. J and I placed our orders, and I told him to go find us an outside table while I got plasticware and straws from a side display. Something made me look up toward the kitchen, and

I saw all the cooks—a bunch of late teen/early twenties Black guys—looking through the round window on the door. They were looking in the direction of where my brother was, so I turned. There was a white girl talking to him, trying to get his number.

I knew that girl. She had been in Upward Bound with me one summer, a program for underprivileged kids to expose them to and prepare them for college life. She was what we called a "wigger" back then—someone who affected Black mannerisms and speech in order to infiltrate a culture not her own. She had long permed hair and spoke in a blaccent and frequently talked about her Black boyfriends. I saw her chatting up my brother and my brother trying to remove himself from her, and everything went red, then black.

The boys in the kitchen had sent her out to talk to my brother in an attempt to humiliate him. They'd seen him acting differently, perhaps one of his stimming moves, or maybe they'd seen him talking a bit to himself, and they wanted to make fun. They'd sent this white girl, starving for Black male approval, with no sense of shame or pride in herself, who couldn't see how they were using her or how awful it was to try to humiliate someone because he was a little different. Just like they had back in preschool, my protective instincts kicked in.

When I came to myself, I was holding a plastic knife in front of her and telling her to go back into the kitchen where she belonged. She opened her mouth, but I wouldn't let her talk.

"I know you. We were at Upward Bound. I know what you're letting those boys in that kitchen do to you. Go back to them now before I figure out how to kill you with this piece of plastic."

J touched my arm and said, "Come on, Nicki. Here's our food." He tried to pull me away. He doesn't like tense situations, and we had taught him not to give strangers private information, so he knew what was happening wasn't good. He was right. The boys in the kitchen ran away when I looked back at them, and the girl hurried back inside the main area of the restaurant. I threw the food away, because I couldn't trust it, and then J and I went somewhere else to eat.

I was so angry and upset that when we made it back to the church group, I started crying. J awkwardly rubbed my back to calm me down. He is not good at touch, but he knows that people like to hug or have some kind of physical contact in moments of high emotion. When we got home, I told Mama what happened and broke down crying again. I wasn't going to be there for J to make sure no one tried to make fun of him or tried to take advantage of him just because he navigated the world differently. I felt guilty about leaving him alone, even though the rest of our family would still be there with him. But I had always been his protector. Who was going to keep him safe now?

Mama assured me J would be fine, but I knew I was letting him down. I wrote a letter to Opryland about that girl and what she had done. I'd chaperoned one of J's classes to Opryland before, so I knew they often had groups of people with various physical and developmental disabilities come to the park. How could they hire someone who would be so cruel and ignorant? They wrote me back and refunded me the money for my and J's tickets. I was not expecting that at all. They also said they had let ole girl go. That's what I'd really wanted. I hope they told her why she was being fired.

———

When I was young, I would say I was going to be a famous writer and get rich (ha!) so I could buy a big house for me and my brother. Mama would ask if she could live with us, and I'd tell her no. As I got older and a little more sophisticated and more into my privacy, I'd say I wanted a large piece of property so I could build him either his own wing or his own little house and then I'd build another little house for Mama.

At my lowest depressive moments, I have at times wanted to will myself to death, but now the thought of dying keeps me up at night because I worry about who would take care of J in his old age if I wasn't there. He currently lives at home with Mama and her husband, and he has a part-time job. He's always been very good at keeping a job—he loves the routine and structure of work. And like me, he loves having his own money. But I've been in a store with him when someone, usually another man, approaches him and asks why he's staring at them. My sister and I have had to hurry over and step between J and this person and explain: "He's special," "He's autistic," "He has special needs," whatever will be the secret code to de-escalate the situation. J is tall—over six feet—and solid. People see a big Black man making unusual eye contact or standing very still (in order to control his stimming), and they immediately became confrontational. Sometimes J can't control his stimming, physical tics or repeated phrases that occur when he's excited or agitated, and too often, people think the worst.

As awareness of police brutality against Black men grew, I became increasingly worried about J, especially as more cases of police killing people who were experiencing mental health crises came to light. Sometimes when J gets off work at night, he stands outside, waiting for one of us to pick him up. If he thinks he's alone, he'll let some of his stimming go, and I'm always concerned someone will call the police because they see a Big Black Man next to a business acting strangely, and the cops will roll up and kill him before he even has a chance to say anything. J took years of speech therapy and can communicate well, but he still stumbles over his words and pronunciations. What if the police ask him something and he can't speak quickly or clearly enough? Are they going to kill my brother out of ignorance? Because we've taught him to be wary of strangers, he'll say no and start walking away if he doesn't understand why someone is approaching him. What if he turns his back on an impatient, trigger-happy cop? The possibilities give me anxiety attacks and nightmares. I never tell Mama because I don't want to worry her, but someone hurting J, him dying, is a fear that tears me up regularly.

In October of 2020, Mama contracted COVID-19 and

was hospitalized for a week. It scared us all. She was sixty-six, with asthma, and it was the sickest she'd ever been. I was living in New York and couldn't get to her in a timely fashion. She couldn't have visitors. I hated the thought of my mother, known for her eye-catching outfits and gorgeous jewelry, a woman who cannot enter a room without all eyes falling on her in praise, all alone.

By the grace of God and a lot of good care, my mother left the hospital with an oxygen tank and began a slow but steady recovery. Her illness had us all thinking about caretaking plans, and it made me want to accelerate my own goals to buy a house and settle down. I don't think I'll go back to Nashville, but wherever I go, I know I want to have at least three bedrooms, one for J if he ever needs to move in with me.

———

I know I don't talk about my brother very often. Mama once asked me if I was ashamed of him. I tried my best to shut that down. I am not ashamed of my brother. He is amazing and the sweetest guy I know. He gives the kindest compliments, making sure to tell us we look good when we get dressed up. When I come home to visit, he always asks me if I'm going to cook anything, and I make him whatever he asks for. When he tucks into his plate, he says, "Mmm! This is really good, Nicki!" and settles in to finish the rest, while my chest fills with pride. He's also thoughtful and will do things like leave a single cookie in the pack in case anyone else wants to have the last one (even though it can be pretty frustrating to go looking for ice cream and see there is a literal spoonful left so no one can accuse him of eating all of it).

So, no, I am not embarrassed by my brother. I get worried that someone will say the wrong thing or try to make fun of him and I will have to hurt them. It scares me to think I am capable of violence, even if it is on someone else's behalf. It makes me think of my father. Even now, I am not sure what I am capable of if no one were to pull me away. I don't want to hurt anyone, but I think my brother is the person I would kill for.

———

One time my junior high school friend Tanya asked what was wrong with J. We were at church, and he was on the floor, giggling and repeating random phrases to himself in a sleepy manner. I told her he was just tired, but it wasn't until years later, as I was drifting to sleep and my brain decided to play a random memory to stir up anxiety, that I realized she wanted to know his diagnosis. For years, as a little girl, I used to pray that God would make J "normal," but after everything, he is my normal.

HBCUs Taught Me

Every October in my childhood, until I could finally say no in high school, there was a Saturday morning Mama made us get up early.

"Y'all need to get up and eat something so we can go!"

It was usually mid-October, and while, yes, Nashville is in the South, we do get cold weather, so my bones often wanted to stay in bed. Plus it was Saturday, when we're supposed to stay in bed as long as possible. (Honestly, Saturday morning laziness was never an option with my mom when we were younger. If she's awake, the whole house has to be awake, too.) On these brisk mid-October Saturdays, Mama would bundle us up and we'd walk through the alley behind our house to Jefferson Street, a historic stretch of road in Nashville, but specifically Black Nashville.

We weren't the only people making our way out of our homes too early on a weekend morning. People were decked out in reflex-blue skullies, bombers, sweatshirts, scarves, gloves, tennis shoes, boots, and everything else. Reflex blue is a rich indigo blue, the blue of Tennessee State University, and homecoming weekend is incomplete without the Saturday morning parade down Jefferson Street. It technically begins at 9 a.m., but you have to get up early to get a good spot. Generations of Black families stretch up and down the length of historic North Nashville, standing in front of Fisk University, a ball toss away from Meharry Medical College, and along the exterior streets of TSU itself, cheering and waving at the band, the homecoming court, dancers, athletes, and everyone else with the privilege of marching or riding in cars and floats. The full crowds on the sidewalks or perched in lawn chairs in parking lots never push or shove. Strangers lift your baby girl or boy up so they can see better. And there's always a collection of hustlers selling food and trinkets, which is why Mama insisted we eat before we came out. She was not buying anything, so we knew not to ask.

For most of my childhood, I was surrounded by this kind of Black community. Even though my parents never graduated from college, we went to TSU football games. Nashville is a college town, but I honestly have no idea what Vanderbilt or Belmont or Lipscomb (the predominantly white universities) do for homecoming, if they even have such a celebration. It doesn't even matter if no one in your family went to TSU. If you are Black and raised in Nashville, you own some TSU Tigers gear and have been to at least one event on campus.

Fisk and Meharry get a lot of love, too, but they don't have a marching band that participates in the extremely important

Battle of the Bands, an incredible showcase of Black college bands and our excuse to travel to Atlanta and dress to kill.

————

There was never any doubt in my mind that I was going to an HBCU (a historically Black college or university). I grew up within walking distance of three major HBCUs, on a street named after Meharry. I went to Fisk for summer programs, went to Meharry for free dental care, and went to TSU for Upward Bound. I was also bused to an elementary school across town for desegregation purposes, and in high school I was one of only about twenty Black students out of roughly 120 total in our class. By the time I needed to take the ACT and SAT for college, I was tired of dealing with white classmates. I wanted to be in classrooms where my presence wasn't questioned, where no one was surprised I knew the answers even as they asked to look at my homework because they'd forgotten to do theirs.

Junior year of high school, I refused to read *Adventures of Huckleberry Finn* in English class, so I didn't participate in the discussion. My teacher tried to convince me of the merits of reading a book that's supposedly anti-racist yet would force me to see the name Nigger Jim repeatedly. At some point in the discussion, Elvis Presley came up (I wish I could remember how, but I'd probably mentally checked out for the bread crumbs leading to that) and I said loudly, "Elvis stole Black people's music." My teacher tried to shut me down, and a fellow classmate, a Black guy, tried to talk over me and say that's not what I meant. It solidified how ready I was for an environment where I could talk about white musicians and other artists profiting off Black people—without being silenced.

So while the majority of my Black classmates went to Florida A&M, I went to Dillard University in New Orleans. It's a small HBCU that doesn't have the same kind of name recognition as Howard, Spelman, or Morehouse, but I knew that it was where I wanted to be. I'll tell you a secret: I had no idea Dillard existed until I saw their table at a college fair. A student from the year ahead of me was attending Dillard. She was at the table and successfully recruited me. Despite full rides from TSU and FAMU, I wanted to get away from Nashville, and away from my classmates. I had a fear that I would never grow up if I didn't get away from the people from my youth. My mom tried to bribe me into staying by buying a new car. It was for her, but if I'd stayed, she would've given it to me. It wasn't enough. I didn't want a new car. I wanted freedom and new experiences.

The teen TV shows made for and about white kids kept telling me over and over that friends stay together forever and newcomers are a threat to your friendship. *Saved by the Bell* and *Boy Meets World* made it seem so cool to follow the friends you've known since elementary school into college life. They also showed how difficult it could be when you start to grow apart and become your own person. But *A Different World*...wow. It not only highlighted how great HBCUs were, but it also served as a reminder that lasting relationships can form when people come from totally different walks of life.

A Different World gave me weekly extended looks into what was possible in Black college life. It was a spin-off of *The Cosby Show* and was supposed to be a star vehicle for Lisa Bonet as Denise Huxtable, but she left after the first season and the show began to focus on the rest of the cast: Whitley (Jasmine Guy), a rich southern belle attending college to find a husband; Freddie (Cree Summers), a peace-loving modern hippie who wanted to change the world; Jaleesa (Dawnn Lewis), an older student who didn't have time for everyone else's shenanigans; Kimberly (Charnele Brown), focused and determined to be a doctor; Dwayne (Kadeem Hardison), a math nerd with a surprisingly tough, protective side; and Ron (Darryl M. Bell), the playboy who just wanted to have a good time. They were all such different characters, but they looked out for each other, even when the foundations of their friendships hadn't solidified yet.

I realized people could have shared experiences even when we didn't grow up down the street from each other. And I wanted that. I wanted friendships I'd chosen and not just those I'd succumbed to because of the circumstances of proximity. While that might make it sound like I didn't like my high school friendships, most of us are all still connected today. I have one close high school friend I talk to almost weekly, and I don't know where I'd be without her, but even that friendship formed more fully after we'd both been away from Nashville for a while and then returned.

I knew I needed to get away from home to become the person I needed to be. Through the film *School Daze*, I saw inside the drama of dorm rooms and the messiness of Greek life. I couldn't wait to have my own experience of frat parties and doing dances like Da Butt. Would there be a musical battle of light-skinned versus dark-skinned women on the yard? There was only one way to find out!

————

Dillard University looked like a plantation, and we students often referred to the trees as "hanging oaks." There were concrete benches with clawed feet up and down the Avenue of the Oaks, which is a pair of sidewalks shaded by large oak trees, connecting the front of campus (classrooms and administration) with the back (dorms and gyms). Because the campus was so small yet open, shaped like the letter U, everyone could see you when you hung out there. At the back of campus, behind the dip in the U, Dillard had a set of tennis courts that had no lights, which meant that was the Lovers' Lane on campus.

My first roommate was from Mobile, Alabama, and made sure to tell me Mobile is actually where what we know as the celebration of Mardi Gras began. I didn't believe her then, and I still don't, but people from Mobile hang on to that tidbit. She was an okay roommate, but she stiffed me on the phone bill we shared (landlines!), so I stopped fucking with her. Luckily, having a boyfriend kept me out of the dorm a lot, so I didn't have to pretend to be cordial that often.

When DJ and I started dating, a couple of girls vandalized

the dry erase board on my door, saying hateful things about why he would possibly be with me, including that I must suck a mean dick. (I think I do all right. It's really all about the passion you bring.) I wrote something smart but low-impact in response, like "Thanks for your feedback. I'll pass along your thoughts when he picks me up tonight." But their comments stung, because it wasn't the first time in my short dating career that girls around me had insulted me because of who I was dating. DJ was the man on campus, and I was no one special. I didn't dress well, which meant I had no money, and I had no easily observable talent, nothing to make me stand out even on a campus of twelve hundred students, so of course the only reason he must be interested in me was sex. Shit like that was one of the reasons I used to say I didn't get along with girls.

I didn't think I'd have to deal with that kind of pettiness in college. *A Different World* didn't show me that anything like that would happen! *School Daze* did, a little bit—I won't lie. But neither of them told me that HBCUs were extremely into respectability politics, and as much as the overall message of the schools was to nurture us in safe spaces and teach us what our whitewashed education didn't, there was also the message that we have to be twice as good because white people are always watching. At Dillard, we had dorm curfews and the girls had to be inside an hour earlier than the boys. I've never been much of a partier, but it definitely interfered with my dating life. When we girls would bring up the inequality to our dorm mothers and other leadership staff, they'd give us the line about how our parents trusted that they would take care of us, and that curfews were there for our safety. It was bullshit.

Girls were shamed for their attire. If they dressed in provocative clothes, people assumed they were strippers or had sugar daddies to help supplement their income. It seemed like girls who were assaulted just...disappeared. The school was so small that there were two freshman girls' dorms, one dorm for all upper-class women, and one dorm for all on-campus boys. There was a collection of duplexes next to campus that older students and other nontraditional students used, but the strict, sexist monitoring of our personal lives led many students to get off-campus housing as soon as they could.

It seemed like students were also shamed for being gay. It felt like church—you could be a gay man and contribute to the choir or help put on fashion shows, but no public displays of affection were allowed. And you should never actually say you're gay; everyone would somehow know anyway, so there was no need to name it. One of the basketball meatheads tried to fight a gay upperclassman who was very proud of who he was. He wore his hair straightened and past his shoulders, and it always looked good because he knew how to do hair, so he was his own billboard. The jock walked by the hairstylist and called him the f-word. Hairstylist said, "What did you say?" The situation escalated quickly, and Hairstylist beat Meathead's ass. The fight launched a wave of gossip, but the responses were to be expected. Most of the women shook their heads, saying stuff like, "I don't know why niggas don't realize gay men are still men, and can and *will* whoop yo ass. They've been bullied all their lives. They will fight back." Meanwhile, the men said basic shit like, "Why does he have to be so flaming though?" Hairstylist didn't live on campus, so he was already barely around for classes, but after that, he showed up even less. I don't remember if Meathead was given any disciplinary action, but since he was on the basketball team, probably not.

Now one thing *A Different World* did prepare me for were rousing classroom discussions and debates. One English professor asked how many of us considered ourselves to be in the poor working class. Most of us raised our hands, but she challenged us: How many of us had parents who were paying for our tuition? How many of us went to private school before college? How many of us could barely get any financial aid because our FAFSA said our parents were expected to contribute most of the cost? It sparked a discussion about race and class, fear of upward mobility, even as we sat in college to earn a degree that was supposed to help us increase our earning potential. It made me think about the need to hold on to something because you don't know who you are without it. If I achieved upward class mobility and left behind the working-class poverty of my childhood, how would it change me? I looked around the room and saw people in brand-name clothes and expensive shoes and purses raising their hands to say they were poor. It made me uncomfortable in an intriguing sort of way. Maybe we all *were* poor, but we also knew we were not allowed to *look* poor. And maybe we were all lying. Sitting in class that day, watching the discussion shift our perspectives, I felt like a real college student, and it made me strangely proud.

My major was English literature with a minor in creative writing, meaning I read many amazing Black authors. We read slave narratives by *women*. Previously, I'd known the works of Olaudah Equiano and Frederick Douglass, but in college, I found Mary Prince and Harriet Jacobs. I'd read plenty of Black authors before attending an HBCU, because Mama made sure we had a steady diet of Black media and I was always a curious child in the library, so it wasn't that I never knew this treasure trove of literature existed. But at college, I wanted to find the writers I didn't know about. I had a class on African and Caribbean poetry, and it blew my mind. Every poem was rich and full and melodic, no matter the structure, and gave me a different cultural understanding of Blackness and the diaspora. Of course, I knew Black people were different all over the world, and that "the Black Experience" is not just a Black American one, but reading a love poem by an Antiguan author and seeing how the island and the sea can complement that love took my breath away. In storage somewhere, I still have all my literature textbooks and a few packets that taught me Black feminist criticism in such a thorough way that when I made it to grad school, I had a far better understanding of critical theory than any of my white classmates, much to their biased surprise. My professors at Dillard, most of them women, most of them Black, laid the foundation of cultural criticism I still use to this day.

Sometimes my friends who went to PWIs (predominantly

white institutions) ask me to tell them about HBCU life and if they really missed anything. My HBCU experience is a bit different than what gets shown on television or highlighted in Coachella routines. Dillard doesn't have a football team, so homecoming was more about crowning Miss Dillard than halftime shows or parades. I was also in a committed relationship the entire time, so I don't have exciting tales of drunken hookups or too many wild frat parties. Most parties I went to were because DJ was DJing, but those tales are fuzzy from falling asleep waiting on him and not from too many cups of Omega Oil. Sorority life wasn't in the cards for me either. I went to an informational once, which seemed to surprise my classmates. I later shared a concern in confidence with a friend who was a member of that sorority. I said I wanted to pledge, but I was worried a couple of people would be petty because I was dating DJ and they had tried without success. She assured me nothing like that would be an issue. The next day, one of the people I was nervous about came up to me and repeated almost verbatim what I'd told my friend, confirming a pettiness I did not want to deal with. Plus pledging was expensive as fuck.

So I can't give people the exciting stories they're looking for. So many memories are "You had to be there" moments, like the time the whole yard went quiet because one girl had pulled out her panty liner and slapped her friend across the face with it, leaving a streak of baby powder across her cheek. No one knows how the argument started or how anyone could stand there long enough to watch a woman root around in her panties before pulling out such an unsanitary weapon, but we all heard the THWAP and then the squawk of disbelief. There was a beat of silence and then cries rang out across the campus: "AW, HELL NAW! GIRL, WHAT THE FUCK. OH SHIT!"

Now, I can tell that story, but that doesn't mean it can happen only at an HBCU or that witnessing how the moment stopped time was the highlight of my four years there. What made being at an HBCU everything I needed and one of the best decisions of my life was how no one questioned my place in the classroom. At Dillard, my teachers and classmates asked me questions to further discussion, not to prove my humanity. We didn't have to code-switch. We were from all over the world, but Black communication blended easily on campus.

After graduation, I went to Ohio State in hopes of pursuing a master's degree and then a PhD in English literature. I didn't know what else to do after college, and people kept suggesting law school or entering academia. Even though I'd always wanted to be a writer and did not enjoy the spotlight of teaching, family, friends, and mentors kept telling me I had to think practically and find a job that would provide security. I thought about going into publishing, but I could never afford the unpaid internships in New York City. Teaching seemed the most accessible job. So grad school and the PhD, it was.

Ohio State gave me a teaching assistantship, and I thought it would be good practice for the inevitable career I didn't want. I hadn't chosen OSU, but my friend K was going, and DJ had encouraged me to go with her so I wouldn't have to start over fresh in the friendship department, especially in a predominantly white environment.

At OSU, in one of my early classes, the TA, a wiry white guy in glasses, showed a short film and asked us to give quick thoughts. I can't remember the details now, but it covered a history of film, and there was a lot of phallic imagery, like trains going into tunnels and rockets blasting off, which, me being me, I pointed out. The TA asked how I knew that. I looked at him for a second, then waved my hand through a weak explanation, because everyone knows what looks like a dick, but I was also flustered. I was the only one he'd asked to explain their analysis. I was also the only Black person, or even person of color, in the room. Later that year, I won a poetry contest, and the director of the MFA writing program asked me to bring in a copy of what I'd submitted. I was thrilled to do so, hoping she'd offer me a seat in the program, because I'd realized my MA-in-literature decision wasn't working for me. She thumbed through my poems, with me sitting directly across from her, confusion setting further and further into the lines of her face the more she read. When she finished, she looked absolutely baffled, and I felt like shit. She couldn't understand how my poetry had won the prize.

At Dillard, I didn't have anyone questioning my intelligence or talent. If someone asked me to prove a claim, it was either to shore up my argument or expose the cracks in it, not prove I was capable of thought. And this is not to say students aren't challenged at HBCUs. We absolutely are, but in ways that are expected in an academic environment. When a friend asked me to explain my choice of line breaks in my poetry, it was to push me into being more deliberate in my creative process, not to make me feel like I could never be as good as renowned white writers. I never had to wonder if my professor was pushing me on an issue because she thought I was enrolled only for affirmative action points. It was such a relief to be in a classroom without having to fight an instructor's racial bias. Everyone steps into the classroom with biases, but at least at an HBCU, you can usually eliminate one.

I went to college because it was what was expected of me, and I wanted to do it, with the hope I'd become a successful writer. There was also a small Whitley part of me that hoped to find a husband there. I wanted to get married, and since I figured you can write from anywhere, I wouldn't need a traditional job. I could stay home. In the fifth episode of the first season of *A Different World*, "War of the Words," Whitley and Maggie (Marisa Tomei, as perhaps the school's only white student) debate whether or not women can be married with careers without the marriage or job suffering. Whitley argues that women could not have both, that their maternal instincts will override their need to work, and that women were meant for the softer things in life. Of course, Whitley loses the debate, but I understood why this southern belle would hold these thoughts. All the homecomings and football games and Battles of the Bands I attended always had couples who'd met at college, married, and had children, who then attended HBCUs. HBCUs created legacies.

I didn't find a husband at Dillard, but I found one of the

best friends and best people I know. K and I would always catch eyes in class as we looked around, wondering if anyone else noticed the foolishness going on, like the guy who clearly never read assignments and thought he could bluff his way through class. But nope. It would just be us two. It only seemed natural that we would band together. During one of our critical theory classes, a student was talking too much in an effort to distract from her lack of preparedness. She was arguing for the wrong reading of whatever text we were studying, and when Dr. M, who was not fooled by the student's trick, quietly tried to correct her, the student barreled on: "I'm a deconstructionist. *I love deconstruction!*" K and I looked at each other and had to look away as we smothered our laughter. To this day, every now and then, when we get together in person, one of us will burst out, "I love deconstruction!"

K is from Northern California. Her mom had gone to Howard and named her after a word she learned in a Swahili class. K met her husband at Dillard, and now they have a son. Legacy.

K had a plan and followed it. She is the pride of Black women Gen-Xers: HBCU graduate, grad school with a PhD, marriage, child, a challenging but fulfilling job that has allowed her to advance and travel. She did not let herself be distracted. I'm so proud of her. She did all the things expected of her with success. We are the roads diverging in a yellow wood. I know she doesn't understand how I walk through life, seemingly with no plan, just a lot of hope, but I feel like our friendship epitomizes what I was looking for when I went to an HBCU. I wanted to connect with people unlike myself and see how I could learn and grow.

We don't talk as much as we used to, and that's my fault. I don't want to bore or disappoint her with the routine of my life. Sometimes, people think that because I'm single and child-free, I'm having countless wild adventures. Honestly, it's me, a book, and my depression most nights—if I'm not engaging in hookups or "situationships" K shakes her head at. Her life is so full that I want to give her space and not make her feel like I'm another obligation on her to-do list. I do miss her. I miss that connection of catching each other's eyes when something off-the-wall happens. For one of our first friend dates, we went to a feminist exhibit that featured artwork made of sanitary napkins and tampons. As we exited the building, there were clotheslines displaying panty liners covered in various art, like landscapes or nude figures. Outside, we looked at each other with wide eyes and said, "Well. Okay."

Because of K, I went on my first international trip. I kept passing up opportunities to travel abroad because I was afraid DJ would miss me too much and I couldn't stand to be apart from him, but when he had the chance to travel to Aruba for a couple of weeks, he was on the first thing smoking. So after K and I graduated, we went to Cancún to celebrate. I had to scrimp and save, and barely managed to get all the money together, and I felt embarrassed by having to work out a payment plan with the travel agent. This was in 1999, before 9/11, so I was able to travel without a passport. All I needed was my birth certificate. I tried to downplay the significance of the trip, saying it didn't really feel all that international since Mexico is part of North America, but inside I was thrilled. The ocean was shaded a turquoise I'd only ever seen in my grandmother's rings. The men yelled "*Morena!*" and "*Chulo!*" at us everywhere we went. We took a day trip by boat to a neighboring island (which is how I discovered I get seasick).

And I got my first tattoo in Cancún with K. We wanted to commemorate the trip and our friendship, so we found a tattoo parlor that didn't seem too sketchy. K's second major was Spanish, and I knew a few phrases. I'd taken French throughout high school and college, and my brain does this weird thing: When I hear Spanish and can understand it, I respond in French. So we were in the parlor with the handsome tattoo artist who smiled at us in flirty condescension. He and K discussed prices, and when he tried to include me in the conversation, I replied in French. He then tried to speak to me in French, but I was too nervous to do it smoothly.

The tattoo place was a single room, every inch of the walls crowded in art. There were no windows, at least none that I could see while we flipped through books and looked at posters to pick our designs. K chose a small sunflower for her left ankle. I chose two hearts overlapping each other—one red, one black—on my right ankle. The tattoo was quick and relatively painless for me. I talked throughout the procedure, but K was quiet, her mouth pressed together like her lips had been sewn into a seam to keep from exclaiming in pain.

She never got another one, but she inspired my second tattoo. After DJ and I broke up, I emailed her a comic I'd come across that showed a Lovers' Leap. The man was looking over the cliff, screaming, "I changed my mind!" She sent me back an e-card with a purple butterfly and the caption "I hope you learned to fly." And now that purple butterfly is on my waist.

———

I try to go back to Dillard and New Orleans as often as I can. I'm a crappy alum, because I don't donate as much as I should, but my student loans are still a menace to my life, so I think that balances out somehow. There are a lot of things I love about Dillard and my time there, but I'm most grateful that it opened me up to the power of friendships with women. When K got married, I was a bridesmaid and I read a poem I'd written for the occasion. She gave me the honor of choosing her child's middle name. When my first collection of poetry was published, she invited me to be a writer-in-residence at the university where she taught, and had her students read my book. I sat in the classroom and listened to college students explicate my work, which had been a secret dream of mine ever since I sat in classrooms at Dillard and watched language unfold in our discussions. When I got back to my hotel room after visiting K's students, I cried, because I was so overwhelmed with how much her friendship means to me, even if I don't show it through more frequent phone calls. Maybe I'll write her a letter on one of my overnight maxi pads, explaining it all, one day.

Scandalous

We call them "auntie songs" now, the old-school soul and R&B songs we used to sing with all the passion our elementary-school-aged bodies had in our bellies. We were too young to be singing those songs, but that's what our mothers, aunties, older cousins, and play cousins used to listen to, with shining eyes and faraway expressions, holding sweating glasses of drinks off-limits to us. If our aunties weren't listening to them as they sat in the kitchen, staring at memories we couldn't see, the radio played them during every Quiet Storm, sometimes with dedications like, "From Denise to that special someone. She says you know who you are." And then Vesta Williams would come on, singing "Congratulations" to the man who married someone else... Or the ultimate side-chick anthem, "As We Lay" by Shirley Murdock, who sings about everything that happens in those moments before your man has to go home to his wife.

There have always been songs about cheating spouses and their lovers, but when women sang them, they tended to be from the point of view of the disappointed and hurt wife. The audience is supposed to take the wife's side. Dolly Parton's unforgettable "Jolene" begs the other woman not to take her man. As listeners, we empathize with Dolly's narrator, a woman so in love she approaches the mistress with compliments and self-deprecation, so Jolene can let go of the man who speaks about her in his sleep. And then there's Shirley Brown's bluesy, confrontational "Woman to Woman," where Shirley lets the other woman know she's not letting her ruin her happy home.

Songs like "Jolene" and "Woman to Woman" highlighted what a woman would do to keep her man, avoided laying any responsibility at the cheating man's doorstep, and made the other woman a Villain with a capital *V*. But I was more interested in the auntie songs, ones like "As We Lay" or "Congratulations," where we got to hear The Other Woman and realize maybe she's *not* a bad person, maybe she's actually a human being with emotions, too. Maybe the Other Woman is in love and deserves our empathy.

We heard the older women in our families playing these kinds of songs back-to-back, and we sang along, our little bodies swaying, until one day, we were adults, and the lyrics, the circumstances, made our bodies sway in too much understanding.

———

After I'd abandoned my first attempt at grad school, I returned to my alma mater in New Orleans to serve as a college advisor. It was a two-year commitment, and about three or four months before it was over, I met a man with a voice made for night. He was a lovely, nerdy thing with a shaved head, to show premature balding who was the boss. He wore colorful Puma tennis shoes and T-shirts with political figures like Che Guevara. He had a few years to go before he hit thirty, but he already had the look of a hip-hop professor in line at Whole Foods.

He had freckles—a sprinkle of joy across his nose and cheeks. The few dots on his lips were clearly targets for my affection. And he was so skinny. I outweighed him by ten to fifteen pounds, but at the time, my weight was still shapely and neat. He would joke about his bird chest, but I didn't care.

I love skinny men. They tend to be overlooked, particularly in the post–D'Angelo "Untitled (How Does It Feel)" world at the time, but they have strength and stamina that I love to take advantage of, while everyone else swoons over gym rats with shrunken dicks and sperm that tastes like protein shakes. Don't get me wrong. I love looking at certain types of hardbodies and have no problem lusting after the Sterling K. Browns and Jake Gyllenhaals of the world, but in real life, I'm passing them over and focusing on the slim ones. (Well, if Jake wants to say what's up, I'd be down.)

But this guy...his voice made me pause midstep. I'll call him Bayard for now. My friend K had volunteered me to act as tour guide (read: chauffeur) while she and a cohort of eggheads were in town for a conference. At dinner, I laughed too often and too hard at anything Bayard said. He slid me a questioning glance after one giggle too many, and I tried to pull myself together, but it was too late. When we went to a club later that night, our bodies kept angling toward each other across the room. We ended up sitting next to each other, our mouths too close to the other's ear, as we tried to talk over the music. We shared a careful dance to "Don't Look Any Further" by Dennis Edwards before the DJ ruined the vibe with Khia's "My Neck, My Back." Around midnight, I'd dropped everyone else off, and he sat in the car with me until the sun reminded us our deodorants had been working for twenty-four hours.

With a muted dandelion yellow streaming through the pink of dawn, I decided to shoot my shot.

"Is there anyone back home waiting for your morning call?" I asked him. He took a long time to answer, which was answer enough.

"Yeah, there is," he finally said. He looked down at his hands, and I looked at them, too. Of course he was involved with someone. Why would anyone like him be single? He was smart, cute, dedicated to knowledge and education, with that voice made for the sweet spot behind my ear, and I'd met him at the wrong time.

We decided to exchange emails, because that was safe. There was nothing wrong with having a pen pal, was there? Soon, we were exchanging pages of text. He'd call me at work and have me crying from laughter. And sometimes he'd call me at night, when that someone back home was out with her girls, and he'd talk to me with that voice saying what his words wouldn't.

When my work commitment had ended and it was time for me to leave, he returned to New Orleans. I don't know what he told that someone back home, but he told me he loved me. I said it back to him. We kissed.

He had the most beautiful mouth—wide and full, with a quick dash of those freckles. He had a very dry wit and didn't smile much when he was trying to be funny, but when I could get him to laugh, his mouth was a beacon of delight. He was a soft kisser, slow and careful. He always wanted to give me room to change the climate of the kiss. Of all the kissing I'd done to that point, I think he was one of the first to make me feel like if kissing were all we ever did, it would be enough.

We'd decided to watch *Love and Basketball*, a movie we'd already seen in theaters but wouldn't mind watching again. Or rather, a movie we wouldn't mind watching as we kissed on my uncomfortable futon. Neither one of us actually liked the movie or its story of a young woman in love with a man who would prefer she give up her talent and hard-earned career in order to keep his ego from being bruised. If this had been any other kind of night, I would've ranted about making yourself small for a man, my still-tender heartbreak from DJ gassing me, but I didn't want any more ghosts in the room with us.

We moved to my bedroom. This was my first real apartment, and I had such cheap furniture. I had personally assembled the black metal canopy bed found in every hood furniture shop, which had to be the way somebody was laundering money, and it always felt like it would fall apart at any moment. I closed the bedroom door, and my cat, Pasha, cried and scratched at the rug, almost ruining the moment. My memory tells me I had candles lit, and that's probably true. I do love me some candles. The light was soft and flickering as he positioned himself above me. Either he was shaking or I was. One of us commented on the shaking, but the memory is as hazy as the lighting in the room. For many months after this night, we would tell the story of it back to each other so much it feels like I've absorbed his memories on top of my own. I do remember the look on his face as he looked at my body and told me I was beautiful before I pulled him down for a kiss. I believed him.

He was engaged to be married, he'd told me. I tried to act like I didn't care, and for the most part, I didn't. I definitely had some woman-to-woman guilt. How could I contribute to breaking another woman's heart, especially after my own heartbreaking experiences with cheating exes? But Bayard and I started seeing each other when I was firmly in my ho phase, and I decided I couldn't care more about his woman than he did. I also knew I wasn't the first woman he'd cheated on her with. I refused to take responsibility for his decisions, but I had no problem benefiting from them.

Shortly after that night, I moved to a new city near Washington, DC, and he visited again. It was a nothing trip for him. He lived on the East Coast. This time, his cover to see me was academic research. It was August 2002, and he was supposed to be in town for only the weekend, but my body decided otherwise, and not in a sexy way. My spleen spontaneously tore in three places, and internal bleeding landed me in the hospital. He called my mother and stayed with me the entire week, even after my family arrived. He cleaned up my apartment and made sure my cat had a fresh litter box.

I'm not sure what excuse he gave for having to extend his stay, but it was probably paper-thin. Bayard finally went home and was married a few months later. He emailed me from the honeymoon, and several months after that, we made plans to meet up again. He left the hotel website up on his laptop, and his wife found a book I'd inscribed with something sneaky. All the little clues she'd been collecting and trying to ignore fell into place. She eventually reached out to me via email and AIM, instant messaging of old. The exact messages have been lost to time and anger, but the gist remains:

What did he tell you about me?
He didn't talk much about you.
Why not?
You'd have to ask him.
Why you?
You'd have to ask him.
Did you use protection?
Yes.
How did you meet?
Through a friend at the _____ Conference.
Why did you do it?
I wanted to.

Do you love him?

I think so, yes.

Do you want him?

No. I'm not trying to take him from you.

Were you good to him?

You'd have to ask him.

Was it the sex? Did you do something special?

You'd have to ask him.

I saw your pictures.

Okay.

Does he love you?

Ask him.

What is it about you?

I don't think it was about me. Not really.

Why did he do it?

Ask him.

Was he good to you?

Yes.

Did he make you come?

Yes.

I ping-ponged between a strange loyalty to him, the need to defend myself, the desire to protect her, and the need to be catty. I wanted to tell her to leave, that he'd cheated before and that if it hadn't been me, it would've been someone else—but I also wanted to tell her that her pussy was trash.

Bayard's wife reminded me of those petty girls in school

who couldn't understand why guys would be interested in me. I didn't have the things I was supposed to in order to be attractive, but I did talk about sex a lot and it was clear that was the only thing they thought I had to offer. I let her have shots. I got in a few stingers, but I let her have whatever she needed to feel better. Even as I stood firm in my need to give myself priority and pleasure, I did feel like I had betrayed feminism and womanhood. In giving myself what I wanted, I'd hurt another woman. I felt guilty, but I would not allow myself to feel ashamed.

Somehow it's never the man's fault when he cheats. We know he's weak. We women have to be the strong ones and do everything we can to keep him happy at home, or if the chance to be the other woman arises, we have to refuse to give in to his advances, refuse to even tempt him. I resent having to be responsible for men's actions. He knew the consequences of the decisions he made, and he made them anyway. I refused to be held accountable for his part in all of this, no matter how bad I felt in the moment.

She didn't understand how I could be with him and claim to love him, but not want to take him from her. He'd taught me that I could love again after breaking up with DJ and he'd made me realize I could be loved, but I was no fool. I firmly believe in the adage "How you got him is how you get got."

And I'm not going to lie. Part of the allure was that I could send him back home. I loved him and I loved being loved again, but I wasn't ready to hop back into a committed relationship. My ho phase was losing its appeal, yes, but I also knew he wasn't the one. I didn't want to take him on just because I felt obligated by our affair.

———————

After the emergency splenectomy when I was twenty-five, I was sure no one would ever want to have sex with me again. I thought I'd have to recycle old lovers who knew I had that gushy and didn't care about a scar.

I poured out my vanities in emails to Bayard. He'd call me and tell me everything he remembered about my body in quiet detail. When it got to the point where I was fully healed and ready to try dating again, he couldn't stomach the thought, and so he came to visit me. He wanted to be my first lover after my medical trauma. He wanted me to find pleasure with him before anyone else. He kissed my belly and touched me carefully until I demanded firmer attention. Then he was gone again.

A little while later, I came home one night and stopped short of putting my key in the door. Something was off. Had I been robbed? The door was still locked and there was no sign of forced entry, but the space in front of my door didn't feel like me. Inside, everything was as it should be, but when I logged in to instant messaging later that night, Bayard's wife pinged me. We had become awkward friends and chatted a few times a week.

If you're talking to me, you know that he's not.
Maybe.
Mm-hmm.
I had to travel for a conference recently.
Oh? Where?
DC.
Hello?
Yeah.
I stopped by your apartment.
I see.
How'd you get my address?
From the emails you sent to Bayard.
I wanted to see you for myself.
In person.
Why you?

I tried to explain there was nothing in particular about me, but I did know what it was. I was a country bumpkin, someone who had bailed on grad school, while he was a Yankee East Coaster working on his doctorate. He could teach me all the things that were old to her. His jokes were new to me, my laugh even fresher to him. They shared a similar ethnic background, each a child of an immigrant parent, and had visited that homeland together; but I am a plain ole American Black woman, born and raised in the South. He had lived in Brooklyn before and taught me New York slang. He described bodegas and sent me mix CDs he made to put me on to new music. I was a different kind of student for him.

When I think back to him and our love, I wonder if he really loved me or loved the newness of me, the "difference" of me. He was a kind and generous man, so maybe he did. I loved him, too, for a while. I think I stopped loving him first. I was tired.

The next year, I'd had a second surgery, and he and his wife came down to visit me. She gave me a papier-mâché butterfly. I still have it in storage somewhere.

After I had recovered, Bayard came back to DC, with his wife's permission. He said she wanted him to seal the closure, but I knew it was a test. He failed. No candles lit the way that night. He was shadowed in blue and less gentle than he normally was. He would usually start off a little too caring, and I'd have to coax the aggressive side out of him. He once said he didn't want to smack my ass because he didn't want me to feel like a porn star. I appreciated his attempt at being a feminist in the bedroom, but I also wanted my ass slapped.

On the night of this visit, he wanted me to remember him. He wanted to take out all the frustration and conflicting emotions he had about his wife becoming friends with his mistress. He wanted me to feel his anger at betraying his wife yet again. He wanted to punish me for being irresistible. And I took it all from him. He had saved my life. He had helped me realize I was not unlovable. He'd made me remember what it was like to take off the armor of casual dating and relax into a relationship, to be comfortable enough to share secrets. So I would take on a little of his pain. It was nothing.

I eventually cut off both Bayard and his wife. She began

inviting me places and wanting to meet up. I didn't trust her. Is that ironic? I didn't think she would murder me, but I did worry that we were entering *Single [Black] Female* territory. She wanted to know more about me, and Bayard mentioned she'd become more sexually aggressive, in a way that was more my style than hers. There was no real point in growing closer to each other. I didn't want a sister-wife situation, and it was obvious she felt I had some kind of spell over Bayard, a magic she wanted me to share.

As for Bayard...I began to wonder when we would ever end. I wasn't sure what he needed, but it wasn't me. By the time I separated myself from him, he had almost slept with someone else during a work trip. When he told me, I think he wanted me to soothe him and tell him what was wrong with him: Why couldn't he be faithful? I had no answers. I couldn't make him feel better. As I'd known all along, his infidelity was never about me.

At the time, we didn't use the word "ghosted," but that's what I did to him. It felt like our affair was never going to end unless I took drastic measures. I stopped answering his emails and calls. He wrote me a letter, and I burned it, unopened. I was tired of the drama. It made for a riveting story with my friends. They would ask for updates and become visibly disappointed when I said everything was over. It made me wonder if we'd been letting the drama push us along, the thrill of two people who couldn't let go.

———

"Everything I Miss at Home" by Cherrelle shows yet another perspective in the prism of infidelity. In this song, Cherrelle tells us the story of a woman who cheats, without regrets, and is grateful to have found someone who gives her everything she's not getting at home. It's a groovy slow jam, perfect for a two-step and eye contact—perfect for a woman who refuses to feel remorseful about receiving love from unexpected places.

Keyboard Courage

I didn't get my first email account until I went to college in the fall of 1995. Of course, it was a Hotmail account. I told everyone my nonsensical username was a portmanteau of my first and middle names, like "nichoand." But really, I chose it because DJ and I had already started seeing each other and I wanted to eventually make it a couples' account.

Whew. I've been holding that secret in for twenty-five years.

Until that point, the internet had been something I'd used to research colleges or to do social experiments, like type in "white women," then "Black women," to compare the search results. For white women, images of celebrities and little blond girls would show up. For Black women, there were tons of sexually explicit content and mug shots. The internet was supposed to be some kind of information superhighway, but it was still built by man (read: a bunch of non-Black people).

During college, I did not have a personal computer. I

used one of the university computer labs to do any typing or research. Well, to be honest, research was still using the card catalog in the library, which was actually really fucking satisfying. The little drawers would either be so heavy and full with cards that you couldn't thumb through them properly without sticking your knee under it to keep it from falling onto your foot and breaking a toe, or there would hardly be any cards inside, so you'd overestimate how much strength you needed to pull out the drawer and end up taking the whole thing out before fighting to shove it back in. Looking for the books you needed was like a Choose Your Own Adventure task. Go here. Now, go there. Back to the beginning. Head to the stacks, leaving trails of white slips of paper scribbled in Dewey Decimals.

Then you'd have to thumb through thick books that smelled like someone else's happiness and find a single paragraph of useful information that you'd photocopy for ten cents a page and write down on the sheet all of the MLA citation info before sticking said sheet into your folder.

And don't get me started on the delicious sound of speeding through a microfiche roll.

Have I mentioned I am decidedly, proudly Generation X?

So, yeah, I didn't really use the internet for much beyond coursework in college. I may have been a nerd who loved the card catalog and the microfiche machine, but I also had a boy-friend and we had sex *frequently*. For porn, we'd turn to the scrambled cable television channels or the dirty magazines our parents had hid poorly. When I wanted to share my writing,

I'd go to open mic poetry nights or print out too many copies in the computer lab to avoid the photocopy fees.

It wasn't until 2002 that I decided to connect to the internet in any real, long-lasting way, and, like perhaps too much of my life, it was all because of a guy.

When Bayard and I started emailing each other, then IM'ing, that's when I realized there was so much more out there on the internet. As a way to be more discreet, Bayard suggested I join an online community he was a member of. He said we could communicate via messaging there. Plus, he thought I might enjoy it.

"There are these forums, like chat rooms, for different topics, like movies, music, even poetry," he told me. "Maybe you can post some of your work there and get feedback. And maybe you'll see me there…"

The website was Okayplayer, home of the Philadelphia hip-hop band the Roots. It had been online since 1999. There were message boards dedicated to different topics, like all things specifically about the Roots, then a general music board, film and television, sports, tech, and more. General Discussion was where any and everything else went. Need new parenting advice? Want to talk about the latest celebrity gossip? Want to make a post about Prince so your married lover could write you a message in reply? General Discussion was where to go. I created a username that was an inside joke between me and Bayard, but when other people asked, I said it was an homage to Prince. Let's pretend it was PurpleMistress.

Because people had already been on "the boards," as we

affectionately called the site, for about three years when I signed in, which is an eternity in internet time, most people already had cliques, which were largely regionally based. The main groups were New York, Philadelphia, DC, Baltimore, Chicago, Detroit, and Atlanta, plus big pockets of users from Los Angeles and the Bay Area. There were people from all over the world represented, but these were the groups that seemed to have the most impact. I quickly learned the technical aspects—how to reply to and edit messages, how to post a new topic, and how to send private messages, which was called inboxing. These days, I might say "Check your DMs" or "He slid in my DMs"; on the boards, the equivalent was simply "Inbox" or "He inboxed me."

Bayard would sometimes inbox me little messages, nothing too risqué, just something to let me know he was online. We'd have harmless exchanges in public. I always tried to talk to people in polite, fun ways, since I was still learning the dynamics of the place. He told me he was not popular and was mostly a lurker—someone who spent more time reading than posting messages. What he did not tell me was that his wife's younger sister was also a lurker, so when she saw us occasionally have public exchanges, it set off some alarms, which she, of course, brought to her big sister's attention. What made our exchanges so suspicious was that by the time she took notice, I had become someone other people took note of. I wasn't one of the cool kids, like the guy named Desus from the Bronx or the funny young woman named Trace from Louisville, Kentucky, but I was fresh meat. And since I was living in the

DC area when I joined the boards, I had met a few people who could vouch for me. I was real, didn't look like a bag of shit, and I talked about sex openly and boldly.

One of the first people I met in person was disappointed when she saw me. "Girl," she said, "I thought you'd be five ten and stacked, light-skinned with long hair, the way you always talk that freaky shit. I thought you'd look like a stripper."

That was a lot to unpack, so I just gave a nervous laugh, because what do you say to that?

(She ended up having a lot of shit with her, and I had to block her across social media apps over the years because of a volatile relationship she had with someone who became one of my good friends. There were real people on the boards, and real people sometimes come with drama.)

Anyway. While Bayard's sister-in-law was clocking our public messages, Bayard himself was feeling some kind of way about my presence on the boards. I wasn't popular per se, but I received more engagement than he did. He had to watch guys flirt with me online. I was taking up space in what used to be his little corner of the internet, and he wasn't sure how to process it all. I was twenty-five, about to be twenty-six and was finally unlearning all the lessons that had said to make myself small so a man could feel good. I briefly thought about toning myself down, but the more I thought about it, the more I realized he had some nerve—a married man upset that his mistress was pulling attention away from him. I won't lie: A small part of me was thrilled at his jealousy. I still loved him, and I understood jealousy as a sign of fear. He didn't want to lose me, but I also recognized he had no right to try to dictate how I shared myself.

And I loved writing on the boards. General Discussion was usually less strict when it came to being monitored for infractions, and people were looser in what they talked about. I felt most comfortable there. People talked about the pros and cons of washing meat before cooking it. Shortly after I joined, a beloved member died by suicide, and it was touching to see so many strangers, both to me and to the person who passed away, come together to express condolences and speak openly about their own struggles with mental health. There was a Black woman who talked openly about her bisexuality. A white woman was an aggressive advocate for anal sex. Parents posted honest messages about raising children with learning disorders. There were ugly fights between people— sometimes because of a romantic or sexual relationship that soured and sometimes just because one person simply didn't like the other.

There was no such thing as "going viral" back then, but if your post didn't go "View all," meaning it had so many replies you'd have to click "View all" to see what everyone was talking about, it was a flop. The rules for the site were that you could reply to as many posts as you wanted but you could make only two of your own posts during a twenty-four-hour period, so it taught me to be judicious about what I had to say and why. Every week, a user with multiple aliases would create a post called Confession Wednesday. People would reply with a list of wild things they did over the weekend, like stealing a purse from the mall or having a threesome, or they'd unload unpopular thoughts, like dissing an album everyone else loved, or they'd take digs at other posters—subtweets before tweets existed. There was an unspoken rule that you shouldn't reply to confessions, no matter how juicy. So if I wanted to share a story about an interesting date I'd had, I'd weigh how much engagement I wanted. If I wanted to just drop the info to get it off my chest, I'd put it in Confession Wednesday. If I wanted to have people ask me questions or I wanted to give a fuller account of said date, I'd make a post.

People created aliases to dance around the two-a-day rule. Sometimes it was obvious who was behind an alias, and other times it became a guessing game. Folks took it upon themselves to investigate and add up clues. Sometimes people used their aliases to be cruel, and sometimes they used them to express a different side of themselves. Some users talked a lot of shit from behind their keyboards, but in person, they were mad quiet and acted innocent as pie.

Long after Bayard's wife confronted him about me, long after Bayard stopped posting and lurking, I remained. I had found new friends and discovered I like being able to communicate without people looking at me. I could take my time to write responses and find the right words. I could double-check spellings or confirm facts without someone growing impatient with me because I let silence into the conversation. Because of the relationships that grew from the boards, I visited Chicago, Detroit, Los Angeles, Philadelphia, and New York—all for the first time. My friend DL in Chicago would have major house parties and invite anyone from the boards who could make it. People drove from Ohio, Michigan, Indiana. If you were in the Midwest and cool, you were there. I would take my camera and try to get as many pictures as I could. Because I had missed out on at least three years of the board members' bonding, I didn't know all the secrets and scandals, so when I'd post the pictures later, I'd inadvertently start little brush fires of gossip as people zoomed in on a couple standing too close in the background of a shot featuring a guy holding up Mardi Gras beads shaped like marijuana leaves.

I had serious intimate relationships with men I met on the boards, and I learned so much about myself—what I could tolerate, what I wanted more of, what I no longer wanted, how to stand up for myself—online and in person. I learned how to deal with trolls, the people who can feel important only if they make you angry or disgusted. Ignore a troll and they will burn themselves out trying to get a rise out of you.

The boards gave me an invaluable education in the entitlement of cis-het men, even in online spaces. Men posted images of naked women or sex acts as their avatars but reported women who did the same to men. (I was reported a couple of times.) The men constantly belittled women in music discussions, especially if it was about rap. One guy started a thread about how turned off he was when the woman he was having sex with began to touch herself. He said he felt insulted. That sparked a huge discussion about women's pleasure versus men's egos, and the ways men tend to watch porn that led to unrealistic expectations of actual sex.

Topics constantly repeated. It seemed like every other month, someone would post "Do you say soda or pop?" "Sneakers or tennis shoes?" "Sugar or salt on your grits?" "Should men pay on the first date?" "Sex on the first date?" Almost eighteen years later, these same topics repeat on Twitter with almost the exact same frequency, with people still bemoaning the frequency even as they answer each time the topic comes up.

Everything I know about navigating social media, I learned from Okayplayer, including when to log off. Users would disappear, and their friends would provide quick updates: "They're okay. Just taking a break." Some people would make "final" posts about how toxic the boards had become and how they were leaving. People would reply with empathy: "Take care of yourself!" Or with cynicism: "You'll be back." And people did return, so much so that members adopted a slogan: NERL, "No one ever really leaves." You may stop posting, but you're probably still lurking.

The boards were addictive. They moved at a quick pace. It was a good place to get news or learn about new social media, like MySpace, Friendster, or Facebook. I learned about Twitter from Okayplayer. I learned about blogging with consistency from the boards. Writing has always been an important part of communication for me, and even though I did not yet have a career as a writer, no matter what I did, I kept coming back to it. On the boards, I learned about LiveJournal, Blogger, and WordPress, and kept a steady number of random blogs for a decade. I'd write messy exposés about my dating life, with characters barely disguised. Every April, for National Poetry Month, I'd write a poem a day. I learned how to write on the internet—the attention span of average readers, the titillating topics that drew clicks. And Okayplayer was the epicenter of the internet for me.

———

Don Imus was some kind of shock-jock radio personality. By April 2007, Imus's career was over thirty years old, rife with drugs and alcohol issues, and he was not the kind of personality I would have ever listened to. I don't care for people whose only talent is offending others, which is what happened when Imus and his producer decided to call the Black women of Rutgers University's basketball team "rough girls," "hardcore hos," and "nappy-headed hos." This team of women had made it to the NCAA championship, a significant feat, and here were two white men, complaining about how "masculine" they looked. After the incident, it was inevitable that many turned to the General Discussion board.

GD had a mix of people who wanted to discuss the situation seriously, the trolls who wanted to play devil's advocate, and those who didn't want to say anything first but merely cosign. Their keyboard courage went only so far. The incident really bothered me, especially as I watched the trolls take up more and more real estate in the post dedicated to discussing what Imus had said: "Those chicks do look like dudes!" "Black people call each other hos all the time!" It got to the point that

I did the unthinkable—I fed the trolls. I posted a 630-word response, a sin in the world of "I ain't reading all that" memes, but I had to get the thoughts off my chest.

> *the larger issue is that no matter what we, as black women do, it will always come down to us being nothing but nappy-headed hoes.*

> *we can save the world, but did we look feminine (and white) while we did it?*
> *did we have a man while we did it?*
> *did we make that man feel like a man while we conquered all the troubles of the world?*

> *women, of all races and cultures, have to deal with this attitude.*
> *but for black women, the notion of femininity is already a sensitive burden.*
> *we are frequently told how emasculating we are for stepping up and doing the work that white women wouldn't/don't do, that our men wouldn't/don't do, and maybe if we didn't do what men wouldn't do, they wouldn't leave, but who else is gonna do it?*
> *so we do it and are made to feel like we're the reason black men leave us.*
> *and because black men leave us, we have all these divided homes, unwed mothers, violent sons, promiscuous daughters, "video vixens," and are a dying race.*

it's getting to a point where young black women believe all they have left is their bodies.
the way to secure your future is to strip; be in porn; be in videos; ensnare a man with your sexual prowess; trap a man with a baby, and when/if he still doesn't stay, continue to give birth to prove your womanhood in other ways.

here we have a group of women—young women—who used their bodies not to entice, but to reach unprecedented athletic goals, and it still was not enough.

our black girls are struggling to find something to hold on to.
struggling to find something that's "okay" for them to achieve.
and we're telling them that there is nothing.
little girl, there is nothing you can do that makes you worthy of the skin you're in.
so at some point, they're going to give up.
like too many of our black boys.

you're intelligent? but can you cook?
you're athletic? but are you pretty?
lesbian? but don't you want children?
focused? but where is your man?

I must admit, I was proud of what I'd said, even though when I look back at the full response, there is a whiff of respectability politics I had yet to shake off. The fact remains that because I was able to have these kinds of discussions that blended pop culture, race, and gender on Okayplayer, I knew my own mind. People mostly came to the boards for jokes and trolling, but it felt good to be vulnerable and honest in the midst of so much noise and disrespect. I was prepared for the upcoming world of Twitter and for my eventual writing career.

I posted regularly on the boards for about seven years before I took the advice of another OKP catchphrase: "Log off, fam." My mental health was deteriorating. The boards didn't bring me pleasure anymore. I wanted to focus on getting better, and I felt like I was using the boards as a distraction. I could've been figuring out my next steps in life, but instead, I was refreshing and scrolling, waiting for a reason to stay online and away from my real life. When I joined other social media sites, I felt pressure to connect with Okayplayers on those platforms in order to show I had no beef with anyone. Maybe I didn't have beef, but I also didn't want to repeat the experience of OKP. I had a tight core of friends I'd met from the boards, and by then I communicated with them offline. Moving away from that intense space of Okayplayer helped me learn to build online boundaries and how to respond (or not) to trolls. I've done a lot of courtesy follows of former OKPs, but I've also implemented another significant catchphrase so that their online presence in my life "goes hard on mute."

Don't Take Roses Away from Me

During late summer of 2017, I met Hal on FetLife, the site dedicated to fetishes and the people who have them or are learning about them. I wanted someone to eat me out on command. His handle was something basic like Good-Likker. My profile was pretty clear: "Curvy black woman looking for a tongue slave. Don't talk unless spoken to." I get so tired of men talking to me and expecting me to think they're interesting beyond what they can do for me.

Here's the part where I assure you I am not a "man-hating feminazi." I am too direct sometimes, yes, and maybe a little too up-front about my desires. Sometimes I take the fun out of the chase. Sorry, not sorry. My romantic life began with serial monogamy and changing who I was to be a "good girl," to prove I was worthy of someone marrying me. I'm over that shit. I don't have to love someone to fuck him. I don't want to open my heart to someone simply because he satisfies me sexually. Just because I'm a woman doesn't mean I have to fall in love with every man I fuck. Everyone has a purpose, and sometimes that purpose is to show up, eat me out, and leave. I don't want to know about your day. I don't care about your job. Maybe I want to know that you don't cause harm for a living, but other than that, you can keep your life story. Most men are not as interesting as they believe they are, and I refuse to give cow eyes to a guy for deigning to speak to me.

Yes, yes, this is probably why I'm over forty and single, but if a man is worthy of my time, worthy to occupy the precious real estate of my thoughts, I won't have to pretend to be interested.

The rest aren't notable beyond the orgasms they can (hopefully) provide. At one point, I chose to be celibate for over two years, and the shit made me a nervous wreck. Like a traumatized cat, I jumped every time someone touched me. I masturbated constantly, and my crotch-watching became far too obvious for polite company. I thought if I grew to know and love myself away from sex and men, I'd find the love of my life, but it didn't work out that way. The Man of My Dreams was supposed to fall into my lap, according to all my married friends and the relationship experts they swore by, but I'm still looking for his ass.

My dick detox left me lonely and hard-hearted. Then I leaned into that hard-heartedness. I decided to take advantage of all the men who approached me with the clear intention of breaking down my walls and walking away. They weren't really interested in me anyway. I was simply a challenge.

It was after I ended that round of celibacy that I began to date unavailable men more often. In fact, the man I decided to end my celibacy with was married and lived in another state. I met Hector through my friend Renee. He was a close buddy of the guy she was seeing at the time. He was short, kind of stocky, with a thick mustache and pretty teddy-bear eyes. I could not stop watching him at the bar where we first met. I told Renee I wanted Hector to knock the dust off. She, in turn, told her guy, and by the end of the night, we were all headed back to Renee's condo.

In the guest room, I had a sudden attack of nerves. My whiskey courage had evaporated. Was I throwing two years of sexual control away for nothing? Then Hector kissed my neck, and I felt my whole body throb to life. He was sitting with his back against the wall, while I straddled him. He sucked my nipples, and I came in such a quick, startling rush that he hit his head against the wall. He gave a surprised, hushed "Oh shit." I wanted to tell him it wasn't really him. My body was short-circuiting from too much sensation after being starved for so long. For the rest of the night, I was a greedy, awkward, gasping mess. In the morning, I felt relief. Not only from the physical release of the night before, but because I didn't have the pressure of pretending I wanted to see him again.

I returned home, and a week or so later, Renee texted me that Hector wanted my number, my email address, something, anything so he could contact me. Renee said he'd asked about me, through his friend, almost daily. She asked me what I did to him. I'd done nothing! I was out of practice, with no special tricks. I didn't know why I was stuck in his mind. (Actually, yes, I do. My cooch is pretty damn good, even when she's been out of commission for over two years.)

Renee gave my info to Hector, and we began emailing each other. He used his work email or would reach out during the day, to avoid detection at home.

> **HIM:** Is it bad that I am in class not paying attention becuase [sic] I am busy having lustful thoughts of you Ms. Perkins? Tuesday, February 19, 2013, 1:03 p.m.

He sent me a stuffed bear for my birthday. He was full of constant praise. But he was married and lived far away. Surely, he could creep with someone else closer. Why me? He said I was unlike anyone he'd ever come across, but I also think he enjoyed the challenge of trying to convince me to come back. I think he wanted me to feel whatever attachment he was feeling, but I couldn't and wouldn't.

Men want the game of turning a no into a yes, even when it makes no sense in their lives, and then they expect me to chase and cry when they're done with me. I've done that before, and it still left me lonely. When I didn't, when I had no problem with them being out of my life, they kept reaching out. It felt like they had a script and kept sending me prompts for the lines they'd written. Coming out of my celibacy gave me the ability to run hot and cold as needed, and too often, I had to be cold to deal with men. The only heat I had was my passion in the bedroom, and for some, that was enough to misunderstand my intentions.

I think I'm pretty clear about what I expect from casual relationships, and when I first met Hal, I reiterated what I wanted: a man to show up and eat me out as long as I wanted, then leave. He wasn't quite a sub, but he had a specific purpose in my life, and I did not want him to step outside of those boundaries. I don't let men spend the night. I wasn't interested in dating him. What I wanted was to bust in his mouth as many times as I could over a few hours. He seemed fine with that. I should have known better.

When we met in person, I didn't do my usual screening. Normally, I ask for a chemistry meeting, where we have a drink and chat to make sure we vibe. The chemistry check has been a lifesaver, maybe even literally. One guy had such an abnormally high voice I could barely tolerate my whiskey, neat. Another guy constantly explained things to me, even reading cocktails off the menu, like I didn't have the same menu or couldn't read. It made me think he couldn't follow directions.

I'd been in New York a few months, and I guess I decided to throw caution to the wind because I invited Hal over to my apartment sight unseen. He'd shared a couple of pictures, but I had no idea if he actually looked like the photos he sent. They were typical man selfies: him in the driver's seat of a car with a baseball cap, some with the camera angled up so I saw his thoughts through his nostrils, but whatever. He wasn't hideous. When he arrived, the first thing I noticed was that he was a big guy—tall, at least six two, and wide, solid like a football player, with quiet, vivid blue eyes. He lived in New Jersey and drove a fierce all-black SUV. He worked in construction and went fishing almost every weekend the weather allowed. Too late, I realized that if we had met first before he came over, I probably would not have let the dalliance move forward. He was a blue-collar man Looking for a Good Woman.

I opened the door, and I could see his face relax into the pleasant shock men get when they realize I don't look like an old chewed-up shoe. I'm no Lupita Nyong'o, but I'm also not the worst thing to see on the other side of a door. He came in, and we sat on the couch. Even though I had no desire to learn much about him beyond the basics, I'm still southern, so I offered him a drink. We smoked (I was already pretty toasted in an attempt to be relaxed), and then he got on his knees. He took off his baseball cap and revealed a wispy comb-over. In his pictures, he had enough hair sticking out the back of the cap to make me think I'd have something to pull. In fact, it made me avoid grabbing his head in any way, because he was sweaty. I don't mind a sweaty man. I actually love the way a man picks up a sweat while we're fucking. It shows how hard he's working to please me, but something about grabbing a wet head is a serious turnoff.

So! Hal got on his knees, and yo. He was amazing. Perfect pressure, speed variation, use of full tongue, greedy moans, slurping, spreading, everything. He knew when to move away from the clit and dip his tongue inside. Recognizing the clit as important is great, but the honey hole needs love too! He gave the right amount of attention to the lips and surrounding area. He was too enthusiastic when eating ass but I got him together quickly. For a while, that's how our relationship went. He'd come over and roll up. I'd smoke while he ate me out, and it felt absolutely decadent. And he would go to town on me for hours. Literal hours.

Not every woman is into head like I am. I know this. One of my friends asked if I ever get bored with getting head for so long. (If it's good? Never!) And one guy asked me how I could only want head, without wanting p-in-the-v sex. I often do want more, but it's been my experience that once men put their dicks inside me, they become more difficult to get rid of. Maybe that's a humblebrag.

So, no. I have no problem with a man eating me out for hours at a time. I enjoy looking down and watching their eyes search mine for approval and instruction. I love the flash of disappointment when I say thanks and usher them out. I should've stuck to my rules with Hal, but I didn't and it brought me nothing but a headache.

When I think about the way he ruined everything with his *emotions*, I get angry—not only because of what he did, but because of the loss of some of the greatest head I've ever received in my life. He would arrange me so that I was flat on my back with my ass on the edge of the bed; then he'd pull up a chair like I was an actual meal on a dining table. He'd get me to come, then keep licking me softly until I'd calmed down so he could start back up again. He once timed himself so he could see how long I could hang before tapping out. If I remember correctly, it was three hours and forty-six minutes. Almost four hours is a long-ass time for any kind of continuous sex, I know, but dammit, that boy was good. *And then he ruined it.*

After a month or so of Hal coming over once or twice a week, he started asking if I wanted him to bring me anything, if I wanted to go grab a bite to eat, and not in a subservient way. He wasn't offering to bring me tokens of his worship. He was starting to like me. Oh no. Not again. This pussy is too powerful. It changes the course of men's minds, even when I limit contact.

I didn't want this kind of attention from Hal, but I was also on a limited budget and, yeah, I wanted to see how far I could take his affection for me. That's not right, I know, and looking back, it's clear I gave mixed signals. I let him bring me col' dranks and let him know that I still eat McDonald's Big Mac meals when under a lot of stress. He took me to dinner and arrived "dressed up" in a polo shirt and khakis. I could tell he'd made an effort. I, too, had tried to look nice. Typically when hookups come over, I'm fresh-faced in a tank top and booty shorts or an old bodycon dress that's too indecent to wear out anymore, so I've turned it into booty-call attire. This time, I wore a cute top with jeans and heels and makeup: nothing extravagant, just eyeliner, mascara, and an extra-juicy lip gloss. Over pizza, he started asking me about myself—what I do for a living, what I did for fun, et cetera, but the big red flag was when he asked me if I wanted a boyfriend. I gave my usual line of "It's not something I'm actively looking for, but if it happens, I wouldn't be mad." I should've said no. He gave me a small smile and nodded his head in understanding.

That big red flag was flapping loudly, but I hoped I was wrong. I hoped I was reading too much into his questions. Maybe my great pussy ego was coloring everything. I began second-guessing myself, which has always been a mistake.

The real problem came the night I called him over to fuck me. I'd had a really stressful day at work and felt like my editor was calling me stupid in her edit suggestions. I'd ranted as much as I could to friends, and then I started smoking. It calmed my nerves, but it also made me really horny. I had energy to burn, so I texted him. I asked if he would be able to handle it if I let him fuck me. He assured me he would. I knew he was lying, but I also needed some dick.

He came over as quickly as he could, considering it took more than an hour to drive from where he lived in New Jersey to Brooklyn. I could tell he was nervous. I think he'd been drinking on the drive over, which in turn made me nervous. I don't like people who drink and drive, and selfishly, what if he got the bad kind of whiskey dick? The kind that made it difficult for him to stay hard. Sometimes, I wonder if I am psychic, but if I am, why can't I win the lottery?

We settled into our usual routine of smoking together before he eats me out forever. And then it was time for him to fuck me, and of course, he couldn't get it up. I tried to suck him to a reasonable hardness, but it wasn't working well enough. I had dry mouth from smoking, and I just didn't want to do it. I'd been fixing editing problems and dealing with a nice spiral brought on by imposter syndrome all day. I didn't want to have to "fix" anyone or anything else that day. He was supposed to be making *me* forget *my* issues, but instead he was bringing his own to the table. He was making me work for my own stress relief, and that's not how any of this was supposed to go. I was supposed to be living my pillow princess life, not acting as fluffer!

"Maybe I could eat your pussy some more?" he asked with his head tucked down. "It'll help me stay hard."

"Okay," I said, but I was doubtful.

As good as his tongue was, I was losing interest in the night, and then he tried that move of rising up like he was going to slide inside me raw.

He hovered above me, the head of his dick close enough that if I moved my hips up, he would've been inside me.

"Is this okay?" he asked, breathless, his voice turned to seduction.

"No, I told you I don't have sex without a condom." I pushed him back and suggested he leave and we could try again some other time, which sent him into a slight panic. I must admit seeing this big barn door of a man pacing and wringing his hands because he'd disappointed me was amusing. It added an extra layer to my power trip and helped ease the sting of his poor performance.

He did leave, but he blew up my phone over the next several days, sending text after text of apology and explanation.

HIM: As far as the condom thing. I would never push you to do something that you didn't want to or weren't comfortable with.

Trust Me

I kinda blamed it on the condom but that has happened to me in the past when I'm with someone new. I get nervous thinking that you might not like it or I'm not good enough for you. I thought about it through the day that you enjoy me going down on you so much that what if you didn't like sex with me. And it happened. I let it get to me and I couldn't stay hard. Wednesday, September 6, 2017, 4:18 p.m.

HIM: I apologize for that. It has nothing to do with you. I think that you are beautiful and have an amazing body and I haven't felt something that tight in awhile. I just put to [sic] much pressure on myself. Wednesday, September 6, 2017, 4:21 p.m.

As I read through his texts, my stomach felt queasy. The red flag I'd been ignoring was slapping me in the face. I didn't want to have to put anyone in check or hear apologies. Worse than disappointing me with his malfunctioning dick, he had annoyed me. This was supposed to be him servicing me and leaving me alone. Now he expected comfort. I put him on time-out. For about two weeks. I told him I had needed a certain response from him and it was disappointing that he couldn't provide it and that he tried to have sex without a condom, which is a no-go for me. He apologized some more, and I relented. I decided to give him another chance.

I don't know if he took anything like Viagra or simply relaxed, but our next attempt at penetrative sex was much better. His penis was a respectable size, and it did what I needed it to do. But he kept pressuring me to go without a condom. Also...being with him that way made me hyper-aware of his size and strength. When I would grow tired or no longer interested in him fucking me, I'd try to push him off or slide away, and he would think I was coming, so he'd press down harder or try to hold me in place, like I was running from the dick. It would set off little panic fires under my skin and warning bells in my head.

Some nights, he would still have trouble staying as hard as he wanted, and he would keep begging me to let him try one more time. I would tell him no, that I wasn't feeling it, but he'd keep asking until I'd ask him to leave or give in and cold-fish it through. I hated myself for that. I was betraying all the strength and confidence I'd built up. It made me resentful. If something didn't go his way, he'd pout, and I did not want any of his feelings. He was giving me emotional work I didn't want or need.

He was also making me nervous. I'd never really experienced this kind of blatant coercion.

ME: This is why I don't like introducing sex because I don't always want it and guys always think they can get it every time. It's annoying. Thursday, November 2, 2017, 5:52 a.m.

You need to understand if I say no, I'm not trying to tease or get you to convince me. I'm 40. I know what I want and what I can handle.

I know you want yours but if I can't do it, I can't do it. Thursday, November 2, 2017, 10:16 a.m.

I told my friends I was going to end things with him soon. I didn't like that he was making me physically uncomfortable during sex and that he pushed my boundaries. I resented that I had to keep softening my anger and concern because I was worried about how he would react. I could feel hatred burning the tips of my fear.

I was becoming concerned that he might force himself on me.

And then he did.

We'd met at the end of summer, and it was now Thanksgiving weekend. I let him come over because I was bored and lonely but didn't want to hang out with friends. He pulled up a chair to the edge of my bed and ate me out for a solid hour before making noises that he wanted to fuck. I reluctantly agreed, and after his first orgasm, he wanted another round.

I wasn't feeling it and told him so, but he kept bothering me about it, rubbing his hand against my leg, saying he just wanted to try one more time. I gave in and let him get on top of me, but he started having trouble staying hard again.

"We should just call it a night," I said as gently as I could.

"You just feel so good, and I want to make you feel like you make me feel. Just let me try one more time." He was whining. I cannot stand the sound of anyone hitting that nasally begging tone. I'm honestly surprised my vagina didn't turn into a tumbleweed right then and there. *And yet*, I figured if I gave in, he'd leave that much sooner.

"Okay, look," I said, sitting up in bed on one elbow to look at him. "It's not feeling good for me anymore."

"Are you sore or something?" he asked in a clearly disbelieving tone. I rolled my eyes.

"No, this just isn't doing much for me anymore. It just doesn't feel good. But fine. You can try again, but after that, I'm done and you gotta go home."

I lay back in bed, and he got on top. He kept sliding out and stroking himself before sliding back in. I eventually pulled a pillow halfway over my face, trying to signal I wasn't really present for the moment, and he slid back inside me for the last time. After a few pumps, he seemed to get a good stroke and thickness going, and he came soon after. He snuggled next to me, and I dozed for about ten minutes before I woke up and told him he had to leave. I don't let men spend the night.

He sat up in bed and started twisting his hands.

"I gotta tell you something."

The room started to turn a dark red around the edges of my vision.

"What?"

He kept stalling, and my voice felt thicker and lower each time I told him to spit it out. Anxiety, fear, and anger were crowding each other.

"You know that last time I was inside of you?" he asked me, his chin tucked into his chest.

"Yes," I answered.

"Don't be mad, but I took the condom off so I could stay hard, and you were feeling so good, I came inside you."

My vision flashed red. I took a breath and demanded he find a twenty-four-hour pharmacy and get me Plan B. I was livid but trying not to have an outsize reaction.

He came inside me without my knowledge or consent.

He was going to let me lie there and fall asleep, hoping I'd let him spend the night.

The need for violence surged through me, but I felt I had to remain calm so that, if this escalated outside my bedroom, no one could accuse me of being emotional, despite his violation of so many of my boundaries.

He tried to talk me out of sending him to the store, claiming he didn't know the area. He wouldn't be able to find a place unless he went all the way back to New Jersey.

"Fine. You drive all the way to fucking New Jersey and then come right back. I cannot fucking believe you." I put on jeans and a T-shirt while I ranted. Naked fighting is for boyfriends only.

Nerve on top of nerve, he tried to confess his feelings for me.

"I think you feel the same way, too, and you're just afraid of giving in to your emotions. You remember that night when you wrapped your legs around my back real high and told me you wanted me to come for you? I came twice, back-to-back, and I'd never felt that before. I know you felt it, too. It was so intense." He was still sitting on the bed, hands on either side of himself, stalling. He was really trying not to leave, which made me even angrier.

"I was trying to get you to hurry up! That wasn't 'feelings.' I was just talking shit. I wanted you off of me."

Verbal cruelty felt like the safest path as I considered again how much bigger he was. I went online and found the closest pharmacy that was still open, and he eventually went to get the emergency contraceptive. When he brought it back, I wouldn't let him inside. He stood outside the building door and tried to simultaneously apologize and blame me.

"Nichole, I know you were feeling something for me, too. Remember when we went to the movies? You said yourself you don't normally do that."

"That doesn't mean I had feelings for you. I just wanted to go to the movies."

"Can I call you tomorrow after you've calmed down?" he asked me.

"No, I don't want to talk to you anymore." I finally looked him in his eyes so he could feel the full brunt of my anger. "I'll let you know if the Plan B works or not. If it doesn't, I'm gonna need you to pay for an abortion. I'm not having your child." I wanted it to be clear. I would no longer soften my words. The hatred that had been burning the edges of my fear flamed high, scorching any kindness away.

If I got pregnant by this awful man, I would have an abortion, despite how badly I still wanted children, even at my "advanced" age.

He finally left but again started texting me sheets of apologies. Pardon me while I put my feminist card facedown, but his passive-aggressiveness and attempts at gaslighting were bitch-made.

HIM: Nichole will you please just talk with me about this. Let me explain myself to you. Can you at least give me that. If I meant anything to you then just let's talk and hear me out please. Tuesday, November 28, 2017, 1:42 p.m.

ME: If I meant anything to you, you would not have done what you did. Tuesday, November 28, 2017, 2:03 p.m.

HIM: I want to start by telling you what you mean to me. Just please give me that chance. Tuesday, November 28, 2017, 2:08 p.m.

ME: I do not want to talk to you. Tuesday, November 28, 2017, 9:24 p.m.

HIM: None of this is about making me feel good. I am probably more hurt over this then [sic] you. Tuesday, November 28, 2017, 9:25 p.m.

HIM: There is so much more to you that I enjoyed then [sic] just the sex part. I would always try to make that clear to you. Ever since the day you opened the door when I met you I was just blown away by you. And everything after that just got better and better. I think that you are so beautiful in every way. I am crushed that I did something that stupid over a nut to jeopardize so much more of what this could have possibly become. Tuesday, November 28, 2017, 9:30 p.m.

HIM: I know you didn't want a relationship but I did feel like it might eventually happen. We are the same age and you never told me how you felt but I was all in. You are independent, beautiful you stay looking good nails done hair done all the time. I seen you as a potential wife 100 I would tell my friends I met my wife. Tuesday, November 28, 2017, 9:35 p.m.

HIM: I am willing to do anything in the world to have a chance with you again. I wanted to tell you that if you forgive me for this it would be the last thing you ever had to forgive me for because I don't want to be without you. I love everything about you. I just keep wanting to know more and more. Tuesday, November 28, 2017, 9:36 p.m.

HIM: I seriously have tears In my eyes rite [sic] now over this. Tuesday, November 28, 2017, 9:39 p.m.

HIM: I fucked up I know. I just wish you could have got to know more of me and see that I am a very nice loyal guy with a lot to offer. Tuesday, November 28, 2017, 9:41 p.m.

HIM: I wanted to do this face to face but I guess this is how it will be. Tuesday, November 28, 2017, 9:46 p.m.

HIM: I wish you would put everything aside and tell me how you felt about me for real. It's not to make me feel better I just want to know. Tuesday, November 28, 2017, 9:48 p.m.

HIM: Are you still up? Tuesday, November 28, 2017, 11:33 p.m.

He started sending me roses and would text me to let me know they were on the doorstep of my building. He didn't want anyone to walk away with them. The first time that happened, I picked up the roses with no incident. A week later, he sent another text with a picture of a bouquet of roses and a bag of McDonald's at the door, warning me not to let rodents get to my food. I was annoyed, but I went downstairs to get the items and he was there. I tried to shut the door, but he pushed his foot inside and began demanding I let him come upstairs so we could talk. Panic was thick in my throat yet again as I worried that this bear of a man would force himself inside and attack me. I tried my best to push the door closed, but he pushed back, so I screamed. I think the scream scared him, because he let me close the door.

Hal kept texting and sending roses and McDonald's. He placed an order via Uber Eats, and the driver texted me to say it was downstairs. I replied that I didn't order anything, that he could have the food if he wanted. Then I apologized for wasting his time, and he said, "It's okay. It happens a lot." I guess a lot of people send apology meals that get rejected.

I didn't want to block Hal's number, because I felt like it was better to know when he was around than not.

I started worrying that he was parking near my apartment building, that he would follow me. I told my roommate, who was rarely at home, a brief outline of what was going on. She liked to leave the building door open, and I needed her to stop. I didn't want her asking me a million questions, so I told her an ex was popping by without permission and she should not let anyone in or leave the door unlocked. She made the appropriate noises, but it clearly didn't sink in, because one night, Hal slipped a note under my bedroom door.

Our apartment took up the entire second floor. My bedroom had a separate entrance, so I didn't have to come through the main part of the apartment. He'd come over and pushed a six-page handwritten letter under my door. Here's a small excerpt, with his spelling and grammar intact:

Nichole

I want to start by saying there has not been a day that has gone by that you are not on my mind. It has been a month since i have seen you. Everything was going so perfect between us. I feel like you were opening up to me and letting me in. I felt like i was doing everything rite to keep you happy.

I wish i did not contact you when you asked. I feel now that you were testing me. It was hard for me

SOMETIMES I TRIP ON HOW HAPPY WE COULD BE

then to see that. I had the emotion of guilt. Something that i am not used to. It's that we were not even having problems. Things between us were getting better and better weekly. I was and still am torn over that night. I just wanted to make everything rite and show you that i didn't want you to think i would walk away on you. I guess i tried to fast and i didn't give you the time you needed. I was only trying to show you how sorry i was. My intentions were never to scare you. I let you know the times i was there. The time i put my foot in the door i just wanted you to hear me out. I am a big guy if I wanted to I could have pushed the door open. You had all your weight on the door and it was squashing my foot. Thats why i kept putting force back. I remember in your texts you saying about me ignoring your wishes. At that time i was so hurt myself and so worried about losing you that i could not see all of this at that time. I was stupid and selfish and not thinking of how you felt. I feel so ashamed that i showed my worst side to the best thing that i have ever had. I enjoyed every second I spent with you in and out of the bedroom. I used to like taking you out because you used to get dressed up and look so good everytime. I did that also to show you that it wasn't all about sex that i liked. It was you.

Nichole since the day i met you, i thought you were so beautiful. I will never forget when you opened the door. You had your hair natural and had blonde in it and i could not believe what i was about to pleasure. Then it started and from what you have told me we were both in heaven. I have never in my entire life enjoyed pleasuring anyone the way i do to you. I feel like everyone i have ever met has prepared me for you. Everytime i am with you i put so much passion into pleasuring you and i have never done that with anyone before until you. I could never get tired of pleasuring you ever. Your taste your scent your soft skin would drive me crazy everytime i have ever spent with you. Our sexual chemistry to me is like no other. The sex we had just got better and better. That night when i started to make love to you by far the best sex I ever had in my life. When I held you and you grabbed me back and with the things you were saying there is just no way you could have not been feeling exactly how I was.

The rest of the letter was him making excuses for what he did:

I could have lied to you that night and said the condom broke. I didn't. I could have said nothing at all and waited it out. If you did get pregnant i could have denied it. I could have just went ghost but i didn't. I admitted what i did because i care about you. I would not have done any of these things to you.

I just wish that you can step back and see the good

in me and all the nice things i have done for you and let them outweigh it…

I don't know your history or what may have happened to you in other relationships but i am one of the nicest guys you will know. Please don't give up on me. I know i should not put this in this letter but if i can just talk to that pretty kitty and tell her how sorry i am she would believe me. I miss you nichole. Please let me back in your life…

This man who had repeatedly pressured me into sex, who had ignored my pleasure to get his, who had violated two of my most sacred casual sex rules, told me he was a Nice Guy. If the stench of emotional abuse coming from his letter wasn't enough to send me running for the hills, the fact that his handwriting looked almost exactly like my father's would have done the job.

I was officially afraid. How many nights had he been driving to park outside my door?

I took pictures of the letter and asked my friend Lola, whose boo thang was an investigative reporter, to go with me to file a police report.

Lola and her friend went with me to the police station. The officer, a white guy with dark, close-cut hair a little too long on top and such a thick New York accent I thought it was fake, made me almost as uncomfortable as Hal. He filled out the paperwork as I answered his questions.

"Race," he said instead of asking, as if bored already.

"Of me or the guy?" I asked for clarity.

"The guy." He looked at me over his glasses. He could've been cute if he weren't a dick or a cop.

"He's white," I replied.

The cop raised his eyebrow at me in assessment and gave me a sweeping glance.

"Do you know his address?"

"Not specifically. I never went there, but it was in near Newark," I told him.

The officer looked impressed and said something along the lines of "Boy, he must really like you to come all that way," and it felt so nasty and scuzzy. I guess he thought he was complimenting me, like "You've got a white boy driving from Jersey to be with you; you must really be worth it." If I hadn't been there filing a report because said white boy had escalated to stalking me, maybe I would have taken it as praise, but now was not the time, copper!

I was scared after filing the police report. Would Hal somehow get a copy and escalate even further? Would this man kill me for rejecting him? Was it all my fault because I'd kept blurring my own boundaries, trying to be nice?

I worried I'd fall out of love with roses. I loved them and enjoyed buying colorful bouquets to brighten up my place. Some people think they're boring and played out, but I'd always appreciated the simple beauty of them, the velvet petals under my thumbs.

And he was ruining them.

The grocery store bouquets would pile up on my dresser. I refused to put them in water, refused to smell them or touch them. They were not an expression of love. Not from him.

He was another man following some script he'd imagined would appeal to me, and he couldn't accept that I was not performing my lines. When he'd asked me if I wanted a boyfriend and my answer was ambiguous, he took it as a sign to woo me, to show me he could be what I said I didn't want. In page 5 of his letter, he wrote, "I know you don't want a relationship and i am okay with that. I just want to be around for one day that you do."

The idea that if you keep showering a woman with gifts and telling her you know her mind better than she does, she'll eventually succumb to your romantic intentions has lasted far too long and gets perpetuated constantly in pop culture. He was following the examples in everything from movies like *Say Anything* to *There's Something About Mary* to the way Urkel on *Family Matters* harassed Laura before finally wearing her down.

From that Thanksgiving weekend until I moved out of the apartment the following April, I worried every day that he would show up. Whenever I left the building or returned, I'd look for his truck. I started dating again around February, and I worried he'd see someone arriving and lose it. Luckily, that never happened. I don't know if he ever received a copy of the police report or when he stopped trying to contact me. I did eventually block his number.

The stress of waiting for another text from him had become too much.

When I moved, I bought myself some roses for my birthday—a beautiful red bouquet of two dozen stems. I felt safe and free. I felt back in control of my sex. No one else was going to make me afraid to say no again.

I Love Niles Crane

In the 1990 *Cheers* episode "Severe Crane Damage," Dr. Lilith Sternin-Crane (Bebe Neuwirth) goes on a talk show to promote her new book, which is all about women's attraction to "bad boys." Her husband, Dr. Frasier Crane (Kelsey Grammer), and Sam Malone (Ted Danson) are in the audience. Lilith uses Sam, playboy bartender and former major league pitcher, as her example of a bad boy. Frasier becomes the example of a "good boy." The host invites them up to the stage. Of course, Sam wins over the audience of women with his flirtatious nature, and Frasier resents his own seeming lack of appeal. Later, to prove he can be dangerous, he picks up a pair of scissors and runs around the bar, yelling, "Would a good boy do this? I am running with scissors!" Frasier's hair, styled a bit like George Washington's but longer in the back, perhaps to compensate for a receding hairline, flies behind him as he opens and closes the scissors, creating a tinny snicking sound to punctuate the foolishness of his male ego.

For the past thirty years, my sister and I have said the line "I am running with scissors!" any time we pick up a pair. It's not often that a show can bring in a new character and have him become a lasting crowd favorite. Frasier Crane, a psychiatrist, appeared in the third season of *Cheers* as a love interest for Diane Chambers (Shelley Long) and to throw a monkey wrench into the Sam and Diane love story. Diane eventually left, but Frasier stayed, lasting past the *Cheers* series finale to become the star of his own spin-off show, simply called *Frasier*. If you ask me to name my favorite sitcom, that is the show I will give before you've even finished the question, and yet, it's not Frasier Crane that makes the show my favorite. It's his younger brother, Niles, as played by David Hyde Pierce.

On *Cheers*, Frasier doesn't have any family. He even says his father is dead, but on the spin-off, he has a curmudgeonly lovable father, Martin (John Mahoney), and his brother, who is also a psychiatrist. Niles and Frasier are so competitive they took sibling rivalry to elevated, snobbish dimensions, like cattily badmouthing each other for an exclusive membership in a gentlemen's club (not a strip joint but a place filled with baby-bottom-soft leather furniture and rich old white men reading newspapers in silence). Most of Frasier's story lines on the show are about him looking for a relationship after his divorce from Lilith sends him across the country from Boston to his hometown of Seattle. When we first meet Niles, he's married to the never-seen Maris, a Seattle socialite too delicate to do anything except shop and pamper herself with expensive beauty treatments. On the surface, Niles seems stuffy and starched, a perfect companion for an invisible woman who wants affection through displays of wealth, but it's through his attraction to Daphne Moon (Jane Leeves), Martin's healthcare provider, that we see Niles is a passionate, thoughtful man— and he has ruined me.

I want my Niles Crane.

―――――

Frasier ran for eleven seasons, from 1993 to 2004. Until I left for college, my sister and I watched the show and fell apart at the seams practically every time Niles spoke. We had watched *Cheers* together, and I pretty much always watched whatever my sister did in order to spend time with her. Mama says we were like two old ladies on the couch, cackling. The television show *Bones* helped pull me from an especially aggressive depressive moment in my life, but *Frasier* is what I use as a regular antidepressant. For a while, I watched my DVDs all the way through once a season, but I realized gorging myself so often was dimming my taste for the show, so now I limit myself to watching all eleven seasons once a year. However, I pop into random seasons all the time and let the episodes run to balance me out at the end of a long day.

It's become a barometer for my life. When I've gone too long without watching *Frasier*, I start to get irritated. I measure the potential in dates by whether they already like the show or how they respond when I put it on when they come over. If they don't pay attention or laugh, I know there's not much they can bring to my life.

———

Niles always wears a suit and tie, oversized just enough to mark mid-'90s fashion but somber enough to indicate wealthy professional. He is so smart and witty; he can cut someone in half with that sharp tongue. I truly think Niles received all the best lines on the show, and Hyde Pierce added a graceful bit of physical comedy to the character that leaves me swooning. In "Three Valentines," Niles (long separated from Maris) gets ready for a date in Frasier's apartment. At the top of the scene, he explains to Frasier on the phone that his date is a fastidious woman, so everything has to be perfect. He's cooking dinner when he realizes the crease in one of his pantlegs isn't as neat as it could be. Niles is very particular about these things, and now he has the added pressure of a date. He begins ironing, somehow cuts his finger, passes out onto the couch from the sight of blood, recovers, tries to get the blood out of the sofa with a special cleaning fluid but passes out again; then his pants catch on fire. He tosses the burning trousers onto the couch where he'd spilled the highly flammable cleaning fluid, which sparks a huge fire, so he takes the big pot of noodles he was cooking and tosses them on the flames, effectively and completely ruining his date before it's even begun. Because

Niles is the only breathing soul in the apartment, other than Martin's dog, Eddie, there is no more dialogue after his phone call to Frasier. The humor comes entirely from Hyde Pierce's increasingly panicked facial expressions and body language. It's a modern vaudeville act, and Hyde Pierce owns it thoroughly. It's one of my top three Niles Crane moments.

Niles is a fussbudget with every allergy known to man and, according to Frasier, can barely lift anything heavier than a nail file, so you wouldn't consider him the most stereotypically masculine of men, but he is also hot-blooded and possessive and incredibly ethical, and he loves Daphne so much, even when he isn't supposed to. I love a good yearning, and Niles Crane is television's best yearner.

As a freelance writer and media person, my pitches aren't always good enough. I see people making announcements about promotions or lucrative deals, and sometimes I feel envious. I wonder where my portion is. Sometimes my Instagram coughs up too many "Happy Anniversary, baby!" posts, and the past ten years of singlehood swallow me whole. I'm not proud of those envious feelings, and I try my best to work through them with facts and tips I've learned from therapy, but the thing that works best for me is cueing up a heavy Niles and Daphne episode, and watching patience, perseverance, and passion win.

Niles was in a strange, affectionless marriage when he fell for

Daphne, someone he never thought he could have, someone who was completely clueless to his feelings. His frustrations frequently got the better of him and he tried to sabotage anyone who expressed interest in her, like the time he told Daphne a contractor who wanted to ask her out had slept with all his wealthy clients, or the time he showed up to a dinner where Frasier had hoped to set Daphne up with his boss. Niles was even jealous of his nephew Frederick's childhood crush on Daphne, because Frederick was allowed to snuggle himself to sleep on her lap. After Niles filed for divorce, which took years to finalize, he had to watch Daphne fall for other men, occasionally comforting her broken heart. He tried clumsily to see if she could see him in a different light, but he knew neither of them were ready for that, so he offered her counsel as a friend. It wasn't the time for the two of them, and as much as it hurt him to realize that, he knew there was no one to blame. Sometimes things have to happen in their own way, in their own time.

When I watch Niles lean in to smell Daphne's hair or how he stops by Frasier's to spend just five minutes with her, despite not knowing if he'd ever have anything more, I see a piece of myself, learning how to bend my dreams. Obstacles, rejections, and envy pop up far too often for my liking.

My hands-down favorite Niles and Daphne episode is "Daphne Hates Sherry." Sherry is Martin's girlfriend at the time, and in the middle of an unusual heat wave, she and Daphne clash. Sherry tells Daphne she wouldn't be so up-tight if she got laid. The temperature is high; tempers are short, and Daphne runs to Niles's place for respite. After Niles recovers from fainting (twice) at the sight of his long-time crush on his doorstep, Daphne wonders if what Sherry said was right, if maybe she does need a good tumble. The air between Niles and Daphne is crackling with possibilities when an alarm on her watch goes off. She has medicine to take, but oh damn—she left it back at home. The two hurry over to the apartment, and Daphne and Sherry make up with a little help from Frasier. Niles blames his brother for ruining his moment, but Frasier reminds him that he could've written Daphne a backup prescription and he has a twenty-four-hour pharmacy across the street from his place. Niles kicks himself, but Frasier tries to make him see that Niles must not have truly wanted to start a relationship with Daphne that way, that subconsciously he knew it wouldn't have been right.

When I am knocking my head against the wall of my professional frustrations, and envy threatens to swallow me whole, I remind myself a better path will reveal itself and take me someplace even more satisfying than I could imagine.

———

I don't know which is cheesier—that regular doses of *Frasier* keep me sane or that I want someone to long for me like Niles did Daphne.

In the third-season episode "Moon Dance," Daphne agrees

to teach Niles how to dance for an upcoming ball he wants to attend after his recent separation from his wife. His date cancels, and Daphne accompanies him, wearing an amazing red dress that strikes him briefly speechless. Everyone at the ball is watching Niles and pitying him, but when he and Daphne dance a tango, the room is mesmerized by their chemistry and grace. Niles, overwhelmed by the moment, declares to Daphne, "You're a goddess!"

It was not the first time he referred to her as a goddess, and it certainly was not the last. Almost every time he called her that, it was played for laughs, until the eighth season, after they were finally together, when Frasier helped Niles realize that assigning such divinity to Daphne was too much pressure and created unrealistic expectations for her to live up to. An important lesson, but even if it was healthier, I must admit I was sad to see his love become more grounded.

Too many of my relationships have been pinned to earth to keep me from having high expectations. Someone was always making sure I knew it could be over at any moment. I learned not to hope for much: not a card on Valentine's Day, not a phone call or text to end the night, not even public affection sometimes. I may not want my man to be as pretentious as Niles, but I want him to think my presence is a blessing from on high. I want him to create moonlit picnics on rooftops for us. I want tropical vacations where we make love on the beach. I want him to believe I'm psychic even though he is a man of science.

I've had a few subs call me Goddess. I allowed it, but it

secretly made me laugh, thinking of Niles, until one sent some particularly naughty texts:

> and ask your permission to cum

> Yes. Don't come until I tell you to. Do you think you can hold on until I tell you to come?

> that goddess cunt is tight

Well, yes. There is divinity here. Thank you for honoring that, pet.

My Kameelah-Ass List

In 1992, reality television changed from watching prank-filled wholesomeness, for the entire family, to watching groups of beautiful young people serve up stereotypes and sex, for the music-video generation. MTV's *The Real World* transformed reality TV—for the better or the worse is your decision to make.

It started in New York, of course: "Seven strangers, picked to live together in a house...and have their lives taped, to find out what happens when people stop being polite and start getting real." There was always the same variation of characters: a very Christian country bumpkin, a blond cheerleader type, a party animal, a player, an angry Black woman, an angry Black man, a queer person. Everyone was always fit and cute, if not outright hot. When the group had house meetings to discuss the inappropriate or questionable behavior of one of the residents, it was often because of something the token Black or brown person had done.

I was newly fifteen years old when *The Real World* first aired, ending my freshman year of high school, anxious for summer and my sophomore year. I was switching schools, tired of the science concentration of my current school. It was a magnet school, where I'd been since seventh grade, and we had to do science projects every year. I could not imagine more of an academic hell than being a poet/book nerd and having to flex the scientific method on a regular basis. So for my sophomore year, I was moving to another magnet school, this one dedicated to the arts. Everyone there was a musician, an artist, an actor, or a writer of some kind. We were a bunch of artsy nerds, so keeping up with *The Real World* was the perfect way for us to stay trendy while both envying and sneering at the cool kids on TV.

It seemed like everyone everywhere was talking about the show. My sister watched it faithfully, and I'd listen when classmates talked about it, but it wasn't really my thing. To this day, I'm not a big fan of reality television, unless it's watching couples who can barely disguise how much they dislike each other buy or remodel a home. Every time I'm in a hotel, I inject HGTV directly into my veins, but any other kind of reality show just gets on my nerves. The editing is often poorly done and distracting. The overreactions and molehills that become mountains give me secondhand embarrassment. I end up wondering if the money is good enough to put up with being fake friends with somebody, but I guess that can happen in any job.

With *The Real World*, it was so obvious that the cast was being coached on how to respond to certain conflicts, and I felt insulted that anyone would think the audience would accept its shenanigans as real. I don't like any kind of media that needs its audience to be stupid to work, but it was hard to escape the drama on this show, especially that of the intimate kind.

With seven young people living in the same house, late-night drunken hookups happened regularly, with someone usually the odd person out. Sometimes it was the very devout small-towner who looked down their nose and told everyone they were going to hell. Sometimes it was the token Black woman who was too busy having an attitude for anyone to find her attractive. One of the most thrilling parts of watching *The Real World* was trying to guess if the virgin would get turned out by the player.

It was probably all that sex that kept an audience tuning in for decades. The Black men seemed to have no issues hooking up, whether with other people in the house or in the city where they all had jobs together, but the Black women (at least in those early years) rarely got to be as sexually free as other guests. When it came to the 1997 season, set in Boston, it was because Kameelah Phillips, future ob-gyn, had a ridiculously long list of criteria (two hundred items!) that a man had to meet in order for her to consider him a viable dating candidate, let alone a husband.

Kameelah, as the "unscripted" previous narrative had already predicted, tolerated no nonsense and was often in conflict with the other housemates. She knew who she was and never felt the need to apologize for it, even if it made everyone else uncomfortable. She didn't indulge in any of the interdating drama that plagued every season. She was a woman who needed a lot of control in her life, and because she was recovering from a string of bad experiences, including abuse, she clung to her list.

Her requirements included having a name with more than one syllable; not having any children already; never having worshipped the devil; and weighing no more than 190 pounds. Kameelah's strict adherence to her list was meaty fodder in my various friend circles. Men dismissed her as being too picky, saying she'd forever be alone. Most women understood her list, even if they agreed it was too stringent, and many admitted to having their own set of criteria, either written in a journal somewhere or held close to their hearts.

By the time Kameelah was on-screen, I was about to be a junior in college. Although it was never made explicit, the idea that I would find a husband while at school seemed to hang over every conversation about my romantic life, especially since by that time, I'd been with DJ since freshman year. I didn't have a list of what I wanted in a husband because my then boyfriend was enough. In my twenty-year-old mind, he was everything I could want and there was no need to think of what was missing. (Author's note: *Gag!* Sometimes I think about how stupid I was and cringe.) That relationship ended after I graduated from college in 1999, and at twenty-two, I worried I'd never find another love, let alone a husband.

When I joined Okayplayer in 2002, one of the popular board members coined the term "Kameelah-Ass List" to describe...well, the checklist women subscribe to when it comes to dating. People don't like to admit it, but we all have a Kameelah-Ass List. Folks need standards! You can't let everyone into your life just because they smile at you.

I was still in my early twenties when I put together my own KAL. Of course, I wrote it out by hand in a journal, but one day I decided to type it up and save it to a portable hard drive. I must've known I'd need to keep it for posterity, known that the act of writing and saving it would be important for my future self. That good ole mythical "Society" tells women we don't know what we want in a partner, and yet when we create a list of what we want, we're told we're too picky, that we should be open to anyone who pays attention to us. So what's a girl to do?

I tried to write out one hundred things I wanted in a husband but gave up after eighty-six. My list had started to feel too obsessive, and I was worried I could miss out on someone really good just because he didn't make me squirt (item 43). I mean, I still kept that item in because...well, it just felt fun.

When I wrote my own Kameelah-Ass List, I had started my ho phase, that part of life after serial monogamy when you realize you have to change your routine to get something different. Up until then, I hadn't known who I was outside of committed relationships. I didn't know who I was when I wasn't someone's girlfriend. So I decided to play the field. I wanted to know what it was like to have a roster of men at my fingertips. For about three or four years, I learned more about what I wanted from relationships, casual and committed, and what I wanted from sex. The sex stuff I would still be figuring out well into my thirties, but when it came to relationships...honestly, I felt like a bad feminist, because I realized I preferred an exclusive commitment. And as a Gen Xer, by the time I was twenty-five or twenty-six, I was still feeling the pressure to be married by thirty. I couldn't get married if I didn't know what I wanted in a husband, so I returned to the list I'd written and began revising it.

I once showed my list to some girlfriends, and they asked how I could ask for so much when I couldn't bring the same things to the table. I was insulted. I'm not asking for more than what I have to give. Black Christian folks are always talking about being "equally yoked," but my expecting a partner to have the same level of formal education as I do, at the very least, is apparently asking for too much. At the heart of it, this qualification is about wanting to avoid insecure men. And every item on my list had a deeper reason (well, maybe not the squirting).

Looking back over it, I can't help but laugh at some of my silliness and note the things I'm more flexible about now. If I ever get married, he doesn't have to be Christian, Black, circumcised, or able to fix cars. Many items on my list were there because they were important to my family or because I didn't want to have to acclimate anyone to my family (#57: has southern roots). I'd amend the idea that he must be Christian to "must have some kind of faith," even if that means only in himself. I don't want my partner to judge me for believing in something bigger than myself, but I don't even go to church anymore, so I guess I can remove #66: attends church with me. However, not being allergic to cats remains.

Maybe I'm not married because this checklist has stayed in the back of my mind. But it's not like I whip it out on every date or anything. Sometimes I do worry that asking for compatibility is too much to expect from a husband. Should I just give up and start planning my Ranch o' Men, a fantasy compound where I keep all the men I'm enamored with and rotate them, so that my favorite at any given time is in the Big House with me? Men say they'd love something like that, being a stud on call, but whenever I present the hypothetical to a paramour, he freaks out at the idea of fucking after other men, even though technically that's what he's been doing all along.

Men are so strange.

Or should I give up on companionship altogether? Dating remains awful. I have a lot of love to give and enjoy expressing how I feel about someone, but when I'm in a casual relationship and want to do something nice for the guy, like cook and let him have some food (not cook *for* him—big difference!), he acts like it's a marriage proposal. I enjoy cooking, but I live alone and don't care for leftovers much. Sometimes I simply want to share the meal instead of worrying about wasting food, so maybe I'll offer a plate. But showing some southern hospitality often sends the guy running, disappearing for a few days or subtly reminding me that he's not trying to settle down any time soon. It's frustrating, and it adds another layer to my defense when it comes to actually letting a man in.

Maybe expecting men to be emotionally fit and mature (item #21) is indeed too much.

For whatever it's worth, I guess I'm still holding on to my Kameelah-Ass List. I don't know if Kameelah herself ever found what she was looking for, if she ever destroyed or amended her own list. I don't refer to it with any seriousness anymore. It's been over fifteen years, almost twenty, since I first wrote it. Since there are many things I'd remove now, does that mean I'm settling—that I'm old and no one wants me, so I'd better take what I can get? Or does it mean I've become more openminded and generous about what my needs are? I'm honestly not sure, but I guess I'll keep holding on to the list, if for no other reason than to laugh at myself.

My Husband

1. Christian

I used to work at a Christian publishing company in Nashville, and one day, one of the editors asked me what I was looking for in a husband. I rattled off a bunch of things, and he said, "There's only one thing missing." I said, "What?" He said, "Where is God on this list?" I stopped myself from rolling my eyes, but later it did bother me that I hadn't thought about my potential partner's spiritual practice, so when I created this list, I made sure to put his religion first. Now, I'm less concerned about him being Christian, but I would like him to believe in a higher power and/or to respect that I do.

2. Happy

I wrote "happy" in response to having dealt with emotionally abusive boyfriends. I was tired of being an emotional punching bag/emotional sponge that was fuckable. Now, I'd change this to something that shows he focuses on having good mental health.

3. Intelligent
4. Talented, with a serious, productive hobby

I cannot be, and refuse to be, the only thing he has going on in his life. Our relationship can't be his only source of joy, rest, therapy, etc.

5. Formally educated, with at least a bachelor's degree

Whew. I've dated guys who didn't have a college education, and it was not an insignificant problem area for them. They frequently brought it up or tried to prove themselves in unnecessary ways, and I'm over it. If I threw out some random fact or said I already knew something they were trying to teach me, they'd ask where I learned it. I'd say college or grad school, and they'd either get quiet or say something a little sharp, like "Well, aren't you Miss Know-It-All." With this, I'm trying to avoid anyone else's resentment.

6. Faithful
7. Honest

8. Physically attractive

I recently went through a phase where I messed with guys I didn't find attractive. I was trying to prove to myself that looks don't matter, but this mission was a failure. I hooked up with a guy who had a huge block-shaped head. It was so hard for me to look at him that he thought I was shy. The final straw was the guy who looked like a metalhead Santa Claus.

9. Black

I'm a little more flexible about this now. I couldn't imagine being with someone I would have to explain the show Martin *to. Dating outside my race has been an adventure, and I honestly have no idea who will be the man lucky enough to lock me down. I just hope he's someone who won't freak out about my hair bonnet.*

10. Physically fit, healthy, and active

This is as much about me as it is him. I'd like someone who will help me be more active . . . but hiking on a first date is out.

11. Reasonably spontaneous
12. Enjoys travel
13. Middle- to upper-class

I'm so tired of being broke.

14. No children from a previous relationship

I don't think I'm suited to being a stepmother, plus I know I'm selfish and I don't want to have to deal with any exes.

15. Good lover
16. Compatibly freaky with me
17. Nice hair

   I love grabbing hair.

18. Wants children and to get married

   I don't know if I want children anymore. I think my uterus is ready to retire, and I really enjoy being able to get up and go without having to work out childcare plans. Children are expensive, and as I just mentioned, I'm tired of being broke. I do still want to get married though.

19. Is my best friend and offers good counsel

   This was definitely me repeating some shit I heard elsewhere. I guess it would be nice if my husband was my best friend, as long as he wasn't my only friend, which is where, I think, a lot of couples' expectations get messed up. I do still hope he will give good advice, with my best interests in mind.

20. Has a good family relationship
21. Emotionally fit and mature

   I need someone who knows how to express himself, who is self-aware, and who I am not expected to fix. Good luck to me.

22. Affectionate
23. Smells good
24. Respectful

25. Enjoys cooking and cooks well
26. Romantic
27. Focused, committed, and disciplined

I have trouble remaining focused and disciplined, so I need someone who can balance me out.

28. Generous

I like being spoiled.

29. Strong—emotionally, mentally, physically

I have no upper-body strength, so I need someone who can carry heavy shit, including me.

30. Is not emotionally or physically abusive

Relationship and family PTSD is real.

31. Gets along with my family
32. Keeps me sexually and emotionally satisfied
33. Pays bills on time
34. Good with money
35. Likes to spoil me
36. No diseases
37. No drug or alcohol abuse
38. Appreciates and respects my talents
39. No physical, emotional, or mental defects

I'm a bit more flexible on this as well. We've all got some shit with us.

40. Circumcised

This was very American of me, but I have since, uh, been exposed to penises that were not circumcised, and I gotta say . . . we should stop cutting off foreskins.

41. No STDs or history of STDs
42. No previous marriages or engagements

I didn't want to have to compete with any more ghosts. But I've since changed my mind about this, as well.

43. Can make me squirt

This is so silly, but if it happens, I wouldn't be mad.

44. Works with his hands
45. Can fix cars
46. Likes and is not allergic to cats

My first cat was Pasha, who I loved to pieces, and now I have Calliope, who loves booty rubs and intense eye contact, so anyone I'm with will need to be able to hang with a cat who needs as much attention as I do.

47. Dresses well
48. Good hygiene and grooming habits w/o being fussy
49. Likes to spend time with me
50. Pushes me to succeed
51. Is not afraid of failure
52. Loves me
53. Likes me

54. Likes nice things but is not overly extravagant or wasteful
55. Believes in and builds a legacy for the future
56. Has a great voice
57. Has southern roots

This was another thing I wrote because I didn't want to have to explain my cultural background, but I've since learned that I enjoy teaching about who and what I am.

58. Has a great smile
59. Has nice feet and hands
60. Enjoys cuddling
61. Gives good massages
62. Sexy

I want to be with someone who fills me with anticipation.

63. Enjoys reading

Ideally, he reads for pleasure and edification and reads books by women without being shamed into it. Bookstore dates are my favorite. Bonus points if he's into poetry.

64. Likes watching movies

I cannot stand someone who thinks pop culture is beneath them. I don't really have a preference for the kinds of movies he's into, but if we have clashing opinions about genres, like he's super into horror and I am not, as long as we can alternate date-night movie themes, I'm cool. But I'm never watching anything with lots of gore or body horror, so I hope whoever my dream man is, he's ready to watch a bunch of film noir and comedies.

65. In my age range
66. Attends church with me
   I don't go to church anymore, so I should remove this.

67. Likes to feel connected to me
68. Not wasteful
69. Works out with me
   Essentially a repeat of #10. I was obviously starting to run out of ideas at this point . . .

70. Is physically able to have children
   Again, this may not be as important as I once thought it was.

71. A willing, happy, and generous provider and protector
   I want a man who's going to look out for me because he wants to, because it makes him happy, not because toxic masculinity forces him to and he's resentful of the role he has to play in the household. If being a good partner is not fulfilling to him, I don't want him.

72. True to his word
73. Gives back to the community
74. Conscious of conserving the environment and community resources
   I need him to recognize we are not the first creatures here and we won't be the last.

75. Will never cheat on me in any way
   Again, relationship PTSD is a motherfucker.

76. Communicates with me openly and honestly
77. Likes his nipples kissed and sucked

What I really mean here is that he doesn't let the performance of masculinity keep him from enjoying pleasure.

78. Pays attention to me
79. Acknowledges me

I've been with men who wanted to keep me secret, and I need a man who loves openly.

80. Moves with me when I travel
81. Doesn't mind the occasional hard times or struggle

Please don't bail as soon as things get rough.

82. Willing to get a vasectomy after we've had all the children we want

Again, I don't know about children, but I still want him to get a vasectomy so we don't have to worry about any accidents.

83. Enjoys sharing learning opportunities
84. Receptive to learning new things
85. Shares interests with me
86. Supportive and encouraging

This is last, but it's not the least important to me at all. I added it after being in two relationships back-to-back in which my professional successes triggered my boyfriends into either trying to knock me down a peg or thinking of their own failures, so their congratulations were weak and sad. One time, when I'd gotten accepted into a writer's retreat, my then boyfriend avoided my eyes as he said all the right words, and the next day, he entered the start of a depressive episode and boxed me out of his life. It made me feel like shit that my good news sent him spiraling. I vowed to myself that I'd never again be with someone who covered my good news in ashes.

The Night I Took Shrooms

I love Valentine's Day. That's probably not surprising, considering my love of romance novels (and heart-shaped earrings, which is a secret only my mother and the most observant would know about me). It's become "cool" to shit on Valentine's Day, to scold people who want big, sloppy expressions of love. "It's a made-up holiday!" "You should tell people you love them every day!" "It's about a massacre!" "You don't have to spend money to celebrate love!" No shit, Sherlock. Every holiday is something someone made up. I'm not sure how people have translated Valentine's Day into the *only* day you're allowed to say "I love you." I've never heard anyone say that. It's like...if you celebrate your birthday, why don't you celebrate it every day? You should be glad you're alive every day, if we're following that same logic, right?

Now I do agree that spending excessive amounts of money is unnecessary, but I think as social media has grown, people give big, ridiculous gifts in hopes of virality. People also want to prove they have someone who loves them lavishly. It's why we have weddings and receptions, baby showers and gender reveals. It's not just a joining of families; it's acknowledgment. It's verification. "I am human and I need to be loved," and all that, like the Smiths said.

From elementary school until adulthood, I've always put more thought into giving Valentine's Day gifts than their recipients did for me. I gave one boy what I thought was the perfect Garfield valentine—that said something about how cute he was—which he promptly showed to his friends, who laughed at me. Sometimes I'd build gift baskets of my boyfriend's favorite things plus something he'd mentioned off-handedly. You know, to show I'd been paying attention to him. In return, I'd get a single red rose and a bunch of baby's breath in red cellophane, bought from a hustler on the side of the road.

When I was dating The Russian, he made it clear he didn't celebrate the holiday because it's stupid American nonsense.

"Vhat is all thiis red? How minny holidays do yu people haff?" he asked me one day after he came back from the grocery store.

"It's Valentine's Day!" I chirped back at him, trying not to bounce in my seat. He clearly wasn't feeling it.

"I don't celebrate thet crap," he sneered, but he kept his eyes lowered, knowing I probably liked it.

"Well, I do," I said, deciding to take a stand. I used to back down and try to prove I was a Cool Girl who didn't want anything sweet or goofy on the day. You know—see how low-maintenance I am? But I no longer wanted to pretend about any of the things that bring me pleasure or make me happy. Yes, sometimes I want a bouquet of luscious red roses and a restaurant date where I wear a red dress.

When the day came around, I gave him an anti-Valentine card that he put on his refrigerator. He made me a cup of tea.

On a day that's supposed to celebrate having love in your life, I've usually been alone, even when I was with someone.

———

I met The Hippie on Bumble during summer 2018. He was such a gentrified Brooklyn white boy: scrawny, beard, long hair. There was one selfie in his profile of him standing on a cliff or maybe some hiking trail. I don't know. There's a beautiful vista of mountains and a periwinkle sky behind him. He's looking, unsmiling, into the camera, his hair pulled back into a bun, his crow's-feet oddly pronounced. He could've been twenty-five or forty-five, but I could tell by his eyes that he knew things. Things that would leave my body a quivering, satisfied mess. So I swiped right and it was a match.

He was from the West Coast and into landscaping and gardening, hiking, biking, and rock climbing, and he played guitar. Add in the long hair and the beard, and the reason for his nickname is clear. He spoke with the measured, unbothered tone of a Berkeley stoner, even though he didn't smoke weed (anymore). He was very laid-back about everything, quick to smile, but he also questioned everything before answering—in a very annoying guy way.

ME: Hey. Have you seen this movie about the couple who bought a farm?
HIM: Why?
ME: CAN YOU JUST ANSWER THE QUESTION?

He was emotionally hard to read. We started out as a hookup situation. I met him at a restaurant bar not far from my shoebox apartment in Bed-Stuy. He rode his bike there. I asked a lot of questions, like had he ever been with a Black woman before, because I wanted to know if I was an item to check off a bucket list and I wondered if he was uncomfortable being the only white person in the place. He looked annoyed, but he answered me. His energy was weird, and his face was very closed-off, beyond the quick frown when I'd ask a blunt question, so I figured he wasn't feeling me, even though I wanted to jump his bony bones. As I prepared to ask for the check, he asked if I wanted him to walk me back to my place, and I knew he was down.

It was maybe a five-minute walk to my building. He was ten years younger and *maybe* my height, although he swore he was two inches taller. (Don't they all?) I'm pretty sure I outweighed him by at least fifty pounds, which was fine. I like skinny men. They fuck like the ocean. Rolling waves of pleasure that take you under and leave you gasping. And this boy…

I let him spend the night. I do *not* let men spend the night. I will kick you out at three in the morning. Hookups are not allowed to see the sun with me: Don't get comfy. You've done what I needed you to do, now good night.

But The Hippie...I fell into a deep, snoring sleep almost immediately after that first round. Wow.

We weren't really compatible. There was the age gap. He was still getting over an ex, and I was rebound practice. I wanted dick on a weekly basis, but he was too busy and I lived too far away for convenient booty calls. I texted more than he liked. He was not a good communicator and definitely didn't sext. He assumed any kindness on my part meant I was falling in love. He didn't give compliments...unless he was drunk or microdosing.

The Hippie would go camping and come back glowing. That's how much he loved nature. One time I was housesitting for some friends in the Catskills, and they let me invite him up. He spent one night out in the woods somewhere, and when he came back the next morning, he looked like he was levitating. It was honestly kind of beautiful. He also came back with a weird collection of mushrooms. We sat at the dinner table, and he flipped through an encyclopedic book on fungi, hoping to catalog the types he'd found. I do not like mushrooms—not to eat, not to look at. They have no taste, and they remind me of death and neglect. Meanwhile, this skinny pile of orgasms goes out and forages for the things and makes psychedelics from them.

The Hippie told me about microdosing, and obviously I

knew about shrooms and the like since the days of reading *Go Ask Alice.* I've listened to "White Rabbit." I'm hip. But my mom had warned me about how that "white people shit," also known as acid or LSD, had messed with my uncle and father, so that's kept me away from anything harder than alcohol or weed.

One of my mom's younger brothers was an artist. He'd gone to school thirty to forty-five minutes outside of Nashville in the 1970s and started hanging out with other artsy students, most of them white. One day, my grandmother got a call to come get him. He'd had a bad trip on something, no one knew what, and none of his so-called friends were around. Supposedly, he never got over the experience and, as a result, became an alcoholic, and he wouldn't take his psychiatric medicine because it interacted poorly with his liquor. I don't think I've ever had a conversation with him. He was the silent uncle who stayed in his room at the back of the house. No one saw him unless he shuffled through, looking like a ghost, into the kitchen and back to his room.

"My brother could draw. He was doing really well. Then he did that white people shit, and he ain't been right since," Mama spat out more than once in my childhood.

When my father had dabbled with drugs, he'd been in the navy, and my mom and sister joined him in San Diego. This was before I came along, but Mama said she tried to get pregnant with me while out there, hoping to enjoy his military benefits and to get him to act right. He'd already been display-ing abusive behavior, but Mama thought if she gave him his own baby, he'd grow up and stop "smoking dope." This was the mid-1970s, and there was a group of "dopeheads," as my mother called them, living in the same apartment building. My father would spend most of his time with them when on leave from the base.

One day (it's always some random clear-blue day), Mama got a call to come see my father in the military hospital. He'd had some kind of episode. When she arrived, my father stared at her like he had no idea who she was. His eyes were wide and scared. She said he looked like he was seeing things that weren't there. He never told her what happened, and none of his superiors would tell Mama either. He was given an honorable discharge and was never the same. They moved back to Nashville, and Mama got pregnant with me. She thinks he had some "white people shit" that sent him on a bad trip and caused a mental breakdown.

"We can't do the same stuff they can. They can take all that acid shit and be all right, but we can't," she told me. "It's just like how white people gave the Indians liquor and it killed them. We all human but we ain't the same."

Even after the breakdown, my father used to do coke. The living room was next to my brother's and my bedroom. Sometimes late at night, I'd hear him snorting, and I'd check under my pillow to make sure the knives I kept were still there. I'd purposefully rusted them, scratching at them with rocks and pouring alcohol and water over the blades before letting them sit out in the sun. I knew if I had to stab him in order to defend Mama from his coked-out, drunken rages,

I wouldn't be able to put a lot of power behind it, but maybe he could get an infection and die from that. (I'd read a lot of historical romances that featured war veterans and battle-field doctors—shout-out to *Ashes in the Wind*[3] by the god Kathleen Woodiwiss.)

I recently had to put my virtual therapy on hold, but it doesn't take a therapy session to know the real reason I tend to stay away from hard shit is because it always makes me think of my father and the pain he caused our household, especially Mama. There's a history of addiction on both sides of my family, and I've spent my whole life trying to break all the damaging cycles I could. I didn't want to risk becoming like my father—or dying over some bad shit, which honestly feels like it would be the same.

It wasn't as if I hadn't had the chance to try it. In high school, a classmate would drop acid in her eye and write some incredible disjointed poetry and prose. Another classmate offered me ecstasy to get me loose enough to take advantage of me. (I declined.) An ex told me all about raves and rolling, but I've always been afraid, my mother's stories never far from my mind. That shit can leave you vulnerable to predators, vomiting, jail, and death. For all the beautiful colors and heady sexual encounters you might have, maybe someone, in

---

3   In *Ashes in the Wind*, Alaina MacGaren must escape the devastation of her home as a result of the Civil War. She disguises herself as a boy and gets taken in by Yankee surgeon Cole Latimer. Her beauty is far too stunning to fool him for long, and soon they are drawn to each other and must deal with a different kind of battle. It's fantastic!

the middle of a trip or in his desperation to go score again, will tie you up in bed and then abandon you all day, like in the movie *Spun*, and you have no idea how you'll be able to get out. I don't want to deal with any of that.

My thoughts about "hard" drugs changed after an experiment in my late thirties. A colleague turned friend gave me some GHB, the date rape drug, which was also supposedly a gay guy party drug. He told me he took it on a monthly basis, and since he was still a functioning member of society, I reasoned maybe I wouldn't have a bad experience with it. Plus I felt like I'd been trying so many new things after years of following all the main rules, which had not given me the relationship or career everyone said it would. I'd taken a chance on exploring BDSM and dating white men. Why not a little G? Fuck it.

He gave me detailed instructions on how to use it—a clear liquid with the viscosity of water—and I combed the internet for all the horror stories I could find. I read the expected reports about men using it to rape people. But also personal essay after personal essay about men who'd lost best friends and lovers to overdoses at sex parties and raves. Too much of it could send you into a coma. I kept texting my friend for clarity: How often do you use this? What does it feel like? What should I look out for?

I was 75 percent sure I'd finally try some serious shit and die in my sister's guest bedroom.

My friend told me to take a specific amount in some juice, so I took nine-tenths of the amount he suggested. I put it in some orange juice and chugged it. My heart was a nervous drum inside my chest. I had water and my phone next to me while I lay on my back in bed. I tried to pay attention to how much time had passed and began to wonder if maybe I wasn't going to feel anything. Then my crotch got warm. My nipples had a pulse. Every erogenous zone on my body felt like a fairy with a surprisingly large tongue was licking it. My entire body grew hot, and a smile spread across my face. I felt very good.

When I get too high, I feel colors. At a party once, after a bunch of layoffs had affected me and my team, people kept pressing me for details and gossip. I was cross-faded, drunk and high as hell, and because all anyone wanted to talk about was reliving this terrible, unpredictable thing, I had to leave. I told the host, "I feel like cracked blue, and everyone is peeling me." Sometimes, when the environment is good, I feel like a gold shimmer.

That evening on G, I felt like a bright, humming green. The pulses of my body drew my hands and fingers, and the orgasm was probably the loudest I'd ever had while alone. I pressed my face into my pillows, even though no one else was home; then I got scared I'd suffocate so I threw the pillows to the floor and promptly fell asleep. My friend had told me not to go to sleep, to try to walk around with the high, but I felt too good, and I definitely didn't want my sister or nephew to come home and find me lying out on the floor.

It was the most restful sleep I'd ever had. When I woke up, I felt a bit of a hangover, like when you sleep too much. And yet I woke up. I didn't die, and I didn't feel some incredible jones to do it again. In fact, I kept the vial of G hidden away and took it only one more time after I'd moved to New York. I think I used even less than what I'd taken before, because I didn't feel anything the second time and ended up pouring it down the toilet. I have no idea how expensive that stuff is, and I hope I didn't get any sewer creatures fucked-up, but I felt like I'd proven something to myself: I could make informed decisions and not be punished with death. I wouldn't turn into my father.

———

When The Hippie was microdosing, he'd send me random, unexpected selfies: pictures of him smiling mysteriously on the subway, cradling his guitar case close, his pupils pushing any blue into slivers; pictures of himself from a friend's art studio, the sun crinkles of his face smooth. He would also become much more effusive and open. In person, he'd talk my face off, and over text, he'd tell me how awesome I was and how he could have such interesting conversations with me.

With the sober Hippie, things were always straightforward, brief.

ME: Do you like ketchup?
HIM: It's cool. Why?

But a little fucked-up and he'd crack open.

ME: Do you like ketchup?
HIM: Oh man. If you have a really good grade of beef and
make a killer hamburger with some good, dark leafy
greens, some onion, maybe like red onion, raw, and the
burger is medium, with some killer truffle fries. Add
some sea salt to the fries, some pepper, and then the
ketchup...*chef's kiss*

When he'd come over, I'd always try to get him drunk.
I'm not necessarily proud of that, but it was the easiest way
to stop him from being so closed-off. If it helps, I was honest
with him about why his whiskey glass was never empty, and
when he wanted to stop drinking, I never pressured him to
keep going. When he was drunk and would text me little
thoughtful things or be much more communicative, I'd call
him out on it, and he'd get irritated.

> Are you drinking?

Lol yes
😳
So annoying that you
know

> lol why?!

> What else do you know
> that you don't say?

> I may not know you to the
> bone but I know you
> better than you want me
> to

> 😂
> Mmhmm

I think he mistook my knowing him as well as I did as *feelings*, and it fucked with him. It was always very clear to me that we could never be more than booty buddies, even as I let myself do things with him I normally don't do. I let him spend the night. I let him meet my friends. I spent the night at his place. I let him have food I'd cooked. (Again, to be clear: I did not cook *for* him, but sometimes, I'd cook knowing I'd probably offer him some. That is *not* the same thing. Sometimes I'd entice him over with the promise of a plate. He had me eating quinoa, which I hate, and mushrooms he had foraged, which scared me to pieces.) I let him watch *Frasier* with me. I even thought about going camping.

I'm telling you: Give skinny men a chance. They will fuck you up.

———

Suffice to say, I felt comfortable and safe with The Hippie in a way I had not with anyone in a long time, so I asked him about his experience with shrooms. He wasn't a sloppy or violent drunk, and when high, his philosophical California stoner joy doubled. He had good energy, and I wasn't afraid of him or concerned he'd try to harm me if he got too far gone. I'd read about people advocating for psychedelics to help those with depressive disorders, so again, I said fuck it. I asked him if he'd be my trip buddy, and he said sure. We scheduled a dick-and-shrooms appointment, and then I realized what day it fell on—Valentine's Day.

I started to panic. Would he read too much into it? Would he think I was trying to spend A Significant Night with him? Would he bail? Did it mean anything at all *subconsciously* that I'd picked that particular day? More than worrying about a bad trip, I worried that he'd run for the hills. A few times, I'd let him read a poem I'd written, and one time, I showed him lyrics to a country music song I'd written while as high as satellite titties, and he'd always ask, "Is this about me?" Ugh. No! That fact that he thought everything I did was about him made me realize we were not on the same level of emotional intelligence, and I often found myself cursing the heavens because of his emotional ignorance. I was so tired of dealing with men who think anything beyond a moan of pleasure means a walk down the aisle.

But, God, the sex was so good.

Anyway, he came over, and I pulled the Band-Aid off to ask if he realized it was Valentine's Day.

"Yeah," he said, next to me on the couch. "I was like 'Oh yeah,' but then I was like 'Whatever.' It's fine. I don't really celebrate it anyway."

Of course.

My friend Lola had told me not to smoke weed for at least twenty-four hours before dosing, and I'd scoured the internet in incognito mode, looking for as many stories about what happens on shrooms as I could find. The Hippie gave me three capsules, and I tried to set a mood with a cool playlist of Kimbra, the xx, Bilal, FKA twigs, Björk, Portishead—music that's difficult to classify but is good for sex and being high. The lights were low, and we were vibing, talking but keeping it breezy. I was trying not to focus too much on searching for the high, because I didn't want to chase it away. The Hippie stood up and went to the kitchen to refill the water pitcher, and I started to cry, because I'd just been thinking how I wanted some water and I didn't have to ask him to fill up the pitcher after he got me some more water. He simply did it. I couldn't believe how thoughtful he was!

How fucked-up was my dating life that a dude being courteous would send me into tears? He looked at me from the refrigerator with a crooked smile and shining eyes, and I said, "Oh, it's happening."

And then I had an orgasm. Every time I felt a wave of euphoria from the shrooms, I came. I started freaking out. None of the research I had done mentioned sexual responses. In fact, The Hippie had told me he rarely felt sexual when on shrooms. He said he was too aware of his organs to feel

212

sexy. *So something must be wrong with me then,* I immediately thought. All the southern Christian atmospheric shame of my childhood welled up, and I concluded that every orgasm meant I was some freaky freak of nature. And it wasn't just the shrooms. *Every time something good happens to me, I want to fuck to celebrate. No one else in the world is like that, right? Why is sex so ingrained into every aspect of my life? I must be an awful person. Am I going to hell? What is wrong with me? No one else in the whole wide internet talked about coming from shrooms. WHAT IS WRONG WITH ME?*

The Hippie held my hand and talked to me like we were having a regular conversation, and said nothing was wrong with me at all. He held me through each wave as I grabbed the couch and breathed and squirmed. He told me my reaction was kind of hot but never did more than hold me during that first crest of euphoria.

I didn't recognize my own voice when I talked. It got superhigh and nasally. I lost my accent. I called my friend Lola, which is unusual because we only ever text, and I told her I didn't recognize myself, and asked could she talk to me so I could get my accent back. But then I felt another orgasm coming, so I made excuses and hung up the phone. From that moment on, she called me Kristy, because she said I sounded like a white girl and it was weird.

Next, I called my friend Lee, back in Nashville. Our friendship was so important to me, and I could feel our connection. We went to high school together but didn't become close until adulthood brought us back home in ways neither one of us expected. We bonded over the special misery you're in but not allowed to complain about when your plans go to shit and you come back home and become the family's errand runner, because you're single and child-free and therefore people think you have nothing to do. We were also both creative women who tried to be "good girls" when we're really magic.

My friendship with Lee was a neon lavender rope humming with power. The colors were happening, but I needed her to help me get my Nashville back. The idea of losing my Nashville freaked me out because I'm still pretty conflicted about leaving home. I love being southern, I love how Nashville has shaped me, and I love my family, but I think Nashville will be my final resting place and that's it. I feel guilty for not wanting to live there anymore, for breaking up my family and making my mother worry about me because we can't get to each other easily in an emergency. So even though people often tell me I don't sound like I'm from the South, I know Nashville still hangs on my tongue, and I never want it to go away.

The tiny rebellions in my life—refusing to go to church, talking openly about sex, freelancing full-time, et cetera—may make it seem like I'm just floating in the wind, but they're how I try to regain control of my life from other people's expectations of me. My father ruined our family life because he could not control himself, and I can't, I won't, be like him.

Losing my accent, becoming an unrecognizable person, made me think I was losing control, but Lee sent Nashville back down the line to me, and I told myself to let go.

That night, I told The Hippie:

"It feels like we're underwater, which makes sense because you're Poseidon.[4] He was a ho, just like Zeus."

"Limoncello. I don't know this word, but that's what I feel like. What is it?"

"You smell like someone roasting a sweet potato over a campfire. A sweet, woodsy flame."

"I feel yellow. Can you fuck me while I'm still yellow? Never mind. I feel orange now."

When I told The Hippie I felt yellow, he took off his shirt, threw it across the room, settled himself between my legs, and started kissing me. When I said I felt orange and wanted to stop, he immediately stopped and pulled away from me but kept his hand on my thigh to ground me, and I thought, "Wow, do I love him?" He didn't try to push anything and responded immediately to me while still making sure I knew he was there for me. The bar for men is in hell: My shimmying brain was thrilled that he listened to me.

---

4   The Hippie had thick, wavy hair he almost always kept pulled back in a bun. It turned blond in the sun, but it had plenty of auburn and brown in it. I don't know what color it was, but I guess you'd get away with calling it dirty blond. I loved his hair and always made him take it down for me or I'd pull his twisties off during sex. One night, we were at his place and we were both pretty drunk. He raised himself over me and tossed his hair back with his hand. In my inebriated state, he looked like Poseidon rising from the ocean, and ever since then, I've thought of him as the god of the sea...between my legs.

He stayed the night, and I smoked as I came down because I wanted my high to last a little longer, even if it had shifted. He gave me another dose of three capsules, which I still have. I'd take shrooms again though, if I had someone I could trust with me, someone I felt truly comfortable with. I enjoyed the experience and…*I didn't die.* I didn't turn into my father. I didn't turn into a fiend. I let go of me and came back to me.

Everyone says you have to trip in nature, and I'd like to do that one day. Maybe go to a beach and listen to the waves. Let my boobs out and eat fruit naked while riding euphoric waves that leave colors through the air. That sounds lovely.

———

By early summer, The Hippie no longer wanted me. I was annoyed and, yes, hurt. He texted me when I was house-sitting for those friends upstate again, so I was by myself with three cats for company. I couldn't gather my girls and go for a piss-and-moan session. He'd been around almost a year, and I'd become accustomed to him. I liked him. It wasn't love, but maybe I'd fallen into a crush with my hookup, even though he never gave compliments. Or maybe I was just trying to hold on to regular company out of fear that no one will ever love me the way I want to be loved, that I'll have to keep dealing with emotionally immature men until the nursing home.

———

Valentine's Day feels different now. I've started to think of it as the anniversary of the night I let go, and not simply a day that underlines my loneliness. It's a silly holiday, and so much of me wants to give up on it, but I can't. Not completely. Like a fool, every time I write out my intentions for the new year, I list "Have someone to celebrate Valentine's Day with," and, like a fool, I forget I am someone.

The Bonnet

In 1993, writer Pearl Cleage[5] published "Hairpeace,"[6] a
funny, sharp collection of stories about her (and others') relationship to her hair, because, as she points out in the piece,
"You can't be a black woman writer in America and not talk
about hair. They won't renew your license and, well, a black
woman writing without a license in America? I guess you
know the penalty for *that*." I don't think I've ever written anything formally, specifically dedicated to my hair, and I'm sure

---

5   Pearl Cleage's book *Mad at Miles: A Black Woman's Guide to Truth* (1990)
    was one of the first works of criticism, if not the first, that grappled
    with what it means to admire the work of a violent, misogynistic man.
    It's a subject that has come up constantly throughout my adulthood.
    Can we separate the art from the man, especially if that man leaves
    his desk/studio and performs heinous acts against women? Ms. Cleage
    has produced a wide range of work (essays, memoir, novels, poetry, and
    plays), which should be a part of everyone's library. I love her.
6   *African American Review*, vol. 27, no. 1, spring 1993.

the Black Woman Writer Licensing Board is sick of my shit, so here it goes...

———

DJ was walking me back to my dorm toward the end of sophomore year. We were standing on the sidewalk leading to the building, but out of the way of anyone coming and going. One girl passed by us, and DJ followed her with his whole head. She was biracial and kept her long, loose curls pulled back in a sloppy, fuzzy my-mom-is-white bun. She was a fun, loud chick, who smoked like a chimney and had a husky, unmistakable voice. On this night, her hair was still pulled back but her ponytail was loose, perhaps freshly washed, because the curls were more pronounced. Other than that, she looked like she always looked—tanned, fresh-faced, and makeup-free. DJ watched her, focused on that ponytail, and told me, "You should grow your hair out like that." I squinted my eyes and said, "We'll see," but the next time I washed my hair, I didn't blow-dry it and straighten it out...or the time after that, or the time after that.

That's right. I started my Natural Hair Journey for a man. I am so ashamed.

Wow. I don't think I've ever admitted that out loud (in writing). The path to self-realization is a journey! Please don't judge me.

DJ wanted me to grow my hair so it would be long, and the best way for my hair to grow was for me to leave it alone, as in no more perms and no more heat. The thought of no longer perming my hair didn't really bother me. Hairdressers over the years often gave me frustrated compliments—my hair was too soft to hold all the intricate trendy styles of the '90s that required tons of hairspray and gel to make them structurally sound. When stylists washed out the perm, they'd tell me, "If I was you, I would just use a flat iron. You don't even really need a perm." They'd try to use as much oil sheen on my hair as they did their other, thicker-haired clients, and my hair would become a stringy, lifeless mess. I'd sit inside the salon for hours to get my hair straight, but by the time I got home, it was fuzzy and shapeless.

My hair was also too fine for all the styles of the moment, beyond a basic wrap bob, which made me look like an Oompa-Loompa. The only style that looked good on me when I wore straight hair was a pixie cut, or as we called it back in the day, the Halle Berry. Shaved in the back, artfully tossed curls on top, the pixie cut lengthened my face and made my eyes stand out.

My hair never grew to the length of the girl's hair DJ had admired. I cut it and permed it again when I graduated from college so it could look nice under my cap. It would've looked nice under my graduation cap even if it was curly, but I didn't trust that. I'm not sure DJ ever realized why I'd started wearing my hair natural in the first place, and I can't remember if he ever commented on it without my prompting him. During my senior year, I was ignoring the writing on the wall telling me the end of our relationship was near. He was growing distant (because he was cheating), and I was resentful of only being known as his girlfriend when I had ambitions and so much more to me than being his woman. I had been afraid to be apart from him for any significant length of time, but I'd already started applying to grad schools away from New Orleans, where he was staying.

So once again, I allowed myself a tiny rebellion, breaking free of expectations I'd placed on myself, and I changed my hair to prove I was my own person. DJ had no idea about my inner turmoil and would not have cared less.

———

For a long time after I started my Natural Hair Journey, I wore my hair in the only way I could style it: a wash-n-go. I leave my hair in a curly fro because I don't have the talent or the patience to do anything more to my head. It took me years and years to figure out that even natural, my hair is still too fine for twist-outs, braid-outs, or any other full-body looks. So again, I decided, "I'm just gonna leave my hair alone and let it do what it likes best—nothing." When I lived in DC, I overheard my ex Will describe me to someone as "big, pretty fro, lip gloss," and I realized I had a Look. I didn't want people recognizing me by my hair. Look at my face. I have distinct features. Tell them I have pretty eyes, a big nose, and a kissable bottom lip. Look at me.

From that moment on, I decided I'd change my hair up as much as financially possible without causing too much damage to my hair. One day you'll see me in braids, and the next month it's a riotous crochet braid style. Here are some afro-puffs, and now we've got Senegalese twists, baby. I love my hair, but pay attention to *me*.

———

Mama's Family (1983–90) was a sitcom based on a recurring sketch from *The Carol Burnett Show*. Vicki Lawrence starred as Mama/Thelma Harper, a tight-lipped southern widow who'd rather speak you out than hug you, but all her insults and abrasiveness hid a loving soul who would do whatever was needed to take care of her family. She wore her gray hair in tight curls, and when she went to bed at night, she'd wear rollers, with what looked like toilet tissue pinned around them, and a sheer pink bonnet to keep it all in place. Whenever she'd appear in her nightgown and bedtime hairdo, she'd have to pause a bit to let the audience collect themselves. ("Filmed live before a studio audience!") People would laugh like it was the funniest thing. The effort women make to be presentable is hilarious. Seeing a woman relaxed and comfortable is hilarious. Look at how unattractive we are when no one is watching, when there's no man to join us in bed.

Clair Huxtable, on *The Cosby Show*, with her husband and five children, went to bed and woke up with her hair looking courtroom-fresh. Whitley Gilbert, on *A Different World*, a woman very into appearances, went to bed with her hair in a looser ponytail than what she normally wore during the day, or sometimes a headband holding back her completely free hair. Later, when she married, her hair was always down and uncovered at night. Sometimes the women on *Living Single* might have their hair wrapped during late-night scenes, but if they did, their state was mostly used as a gag.

On local news, if a reporter turned the camera to a Black woman in a bonnet, you knew she was about to say something ridiculous. Reporters chose these women to add local flavor, but it set them up to be mocked and dismissed. Every night at home, I saw my mother and sister cover their hair to protect it during sleep (and eventually, when I was old enough, I did this myself), and on every screen, it was a joke. Look at how funny-looking women are when they're not trying.

The vulnerability of being unpretty in the comfort of your home is unwelcome, laughable, and yet it also speaks to an intimacy only a special few are allowed to witness. When I lived with roommates or family, the bonnet was unremarkable, because it was something we all wore and grew up with. When boyfriends started spending the night with me, I'd wear my bonnet to bed, because that's part of being vulnerable with someone, letting them see you at all levels of yourself. I can also admit it was kind of a test. If they complained about it or avoided physical intimacy because of it, that let me know I could never be fully myself with them. One boyfriend loved trying to fuck me so hard the bonnet would slide off. Another flat-out told me it made him think of maids and mammies. Wearing a bonnet is not the worst look I'll ever have, but maybe it's not the best, and if you want the privilege of being with me in the dark of night, you need to accept me, bonnet and all. Still, the fear of being laughed at, of being expected to be presentable at all time remains.

When I wore my hair straight, it was thin and lifeless. Now it is thick and full, and when I lie down or press my head against a car headrest or the back of the couch, my hair flattens and stays that way until I pick it back out for volume. That means when I get up out of bed in the morning or after sex, my hair is pushed into all sorts of wild shapes. It's not very pretty. In fact, sometimes it can be downright funny, and I don't always want anyone to see me like that.

Sometimes I post selfies while I'm wearing my bonnet, but I crop the picture so it's not fully seen. When I receive deliveries, I quickly pull it off and fluff my hair, then put it back on as soon as I close the door. I want to normalize seeing women in their protective gear so people can understand that women still exist and deserve respect even when they're "unpretty," but it's hard to let go.

A couple of months back, I wore my bonnet while on a video call with my psychiatrist and she didn't blink an eye. I'm learning how to be vulnerable and protected at the same time.

How to Build a Man-Made Tourist Attraction

Cranberry pills.
D-mannose powder.
No red meat.
Raw cranberry juice.
Pineapple juice.
Water.
Water.
Water.

Men tell me that when I come, I taste like water. It can be sweet or salty or tangy or sharp, depending on the man, his vocabulary, where I am in my cycle, or if I had a steak that day. Sometimes they say it tastes clear. I like this description best. It is not a flavor; it's an impression.

A vision.

When a man's face is between my legs, when his mouth is doing particularly good work, when I start to hold my breath so I can hear every lap of his tongue, I imagine myself as a waterfall. I want to gush into his mouth. I want to catch him unaware, despite his full knowledge that I am a waterfall. I want to come in his mouth and make him pull away, gasping, before he brushes his hair back or wipes his face and moves back into me.

So when someone tells me I taste clear, I wonder if I've sent the vision of my waterfall into him. Does that mean we're connected? Should I think of houses with wraparound porches and matching rocking chairs when I start to come so that he tastes forever with me, too?

No. No man can see into my head, even at such a moment when I feel free and violent, a crashing body of sensation that people approach in careful steps, unsure but wanting.

Everyone loves a waterfall.

Call It by Its Name

It was at a party.

Before the party, I would tell people I'd never suffered from sexual assault beyond the usual street harassment. I mean, of course, I'd felt threatened. I'm a woman. I'd had perverted men masturbate at me on the street and on the bus when I was a child. I'd been afraid to walk past a group of men on the sidewalk. But I'd never been attacked. I thought it meant I'd escaped serious violence. I thought this made me special.

Henry had been to my place before. It had been just the two of us. We'd smoked some weed and had a few drinks, but there was nothing awkward or tense about his being there. We got high and watched television, and that was it. I never felt like I needed to be on guard with him, even after the flirting started.

Let's be clear: I was not interested. He wasn't my physical

type, but I liked him as a person, as a friend, so I didn't do more to reject him. The innuendos he made were something I dismissed as what guys do. I watched *When Harry Met Sally* at least twice a year. I know there are some people who still debate whether straight men and women can be friends. Almost all of my guy friends would cast out a slick remark to see if I'd take the bait. Men always have to check the temperature of the relationship somehow. It was something I felt accustomed to and thought I knew how to handle.

I'd respond to Henry's boldness via chat with an "lol" or a smiley face, hoping my lukewarm response was deterrent enough. I also didn't hide the fact that I was interested in his friend Will. I went out of my way to talk about how much I wanted Will, even going so far as to ask Henry to help me talk to him.

In moments of loneliness and self-doubt, I admit I talked a little shit to Henry. I'd explain why exes were so eager to get back in my pants or throw a flirtatious remark, quickly return-ing to vague comments when I sensed I'd said too much. I was concerned that he'd report back to Will and ruin my chances. I didn't want either of them to think I could be passed around like a blunt. I knew who I wanted, and it was clear to all of us. At least, I thought it was clear.

Because I speak so freely about sex and want to make sure my friends enjoy themselves, I would share favorite porn clips with them, male and female, including Henry. Sometimes he'd try to get a response from me. When we'd talk on the phone, he'd say certain dirty phrases he knew I liked just to see how

I'd react. I gave in a couple of times, telling him I liked his husky voice, before I pulled back, again worried he'd share my slipups with Will.

A few months after I turned twenty-six, some friends were hosting a party at their house. Henry wasn't there at first, but Will was. We shared a chair at the dining table. Everyone saw us. I can still remember how warm he was against my back, his hand at my waist. In the kitchen, by the bar, I flashed a recent scar on my belly to everyone around, and Will paid careful attention. I wanted him to touch me.

When Henry arrived, he and a woman managed to find themselves next to each other throughout the night, but he kept an eye on me. I didn't think much of it. A couple of other guys were watching me, too. It was a house full of beautiful women. The men were watching us all.

I was going upstairs to use the restroom when Henry stopped me. I was drunk and didn't stop the kiss he gave me, but I pulled away before he wanted it to end. I didn't want anyone to see us, and I didn't want him to think anything was going to happen. I'd painted myself into a corner, though, because I'd never flat out told him his flirting made me uncomfortable. I should've been more explicit, but I didn't know how to tell him to stop without losing him completely as a friend.

For too long, I'd been relying on the hope that he'd recognize my lack of enthusiasm at his advances and give up.

The party went on until the police came to shut it down. As Will was leaving with his ride, he gave me his home address, which several people overheard. Everyone knew Will and I were building something. *Everyone* knew.

I was spending the night at the hosts' house, on the sofa in the living room. No matter how badly I wanted to go home with Will, I didn't have a sure way of getting back, and I was far too drunk and high to make it over there. I didn't even change clothes before I stumbled to the couch and passed out.

Henry claimed he was too drunk to drive home.

I woke up to find him pulling down my jeans and kissing me, telling me he wanted to eat me out. My arms and legs were noodles, my head heavy. He went down on me, then tried to fuck me, but I managed to squirm away. He put his dick in my mouth, but I turned my head, so he put his face between my legs again. The room rocked back and forth, and I was afraid I'd throw up. I try my best to avoid vomiting. To me, it signals a loss of control.

He later told me I had an orgasm. I'm not sure if I did. I think he stroked himself to a finish, but I don't remember. I woke up clothed, sunlight weakly breaking through the curtains to tap against my skull. Henry was gone.

I didn't like what had happened, but I had no words for it. Henry was my friend. I'd flirted with him, and we had kissed. He was a good guy, fun and generous. No one would believe me if I said something nonconsensual had happened. I was the woman who talked about sex all the time. I made it a point to go after who I wanted. No one would believe that anyone would *take* sex from me when I was so openminded about giving it away.

Right?

So I tried to keep it cool, to get out in front of it. I told the party hosts that Henry and I had fooled around on their couch but that I was so drunk I didn't really remember anything. That was mostly true. I stayed friends with Henry. We're still friends of a sort. He continued to flirt and remind me of that night like it had been consensual. Even after I had an established relationship with Will, Henry would drop reminders—only to me.

He'd tell me how my stomach trembled as I came, and I'd wonder if that was when I almost threw up. I never confronted him about what happened, but when he'd try to flirt, my rejection was strong. He'd ask me why I never let sex between us happen again, and I'd brush the night off or say the moment had passed. I just couldn't bring myself to come out and say that it was something I never wanted. I felt trapped by niceness, by my misinterpreted reputation, by a man not knowing that flirting wasn't enough of a reason for him to start peeling the jeans off an unconscious woman.

Shame and embarrassment made me avoid the subject of that night completely. I was a statistic, and a clichéd one at that: drunk girl at a party. I thought I had been safe.

I'd been able to keep him from penetrating me, so I told myself maybe what he'd done wasn't worth the confrontation. There was no bruising, no attack, no physical violence that left any marks behind. That night must not have been so bad if I wanted to put it behind me and keep him as a friend, right?

That's how I excused myself from confronting it, with him

or myself. Until ten years later. I was at a holiday party in my hometown. Another party, more drunkenness. I told the story about my noodle legs and Henry, and my friend Lee was horrified. Seeing the look on her face as I lightly recounted what I could remember, I was suddenly hit by the severity of the events. I blurted out, "Oh my God, that was rape," then began to laugh with hysterical panic. I had never said it, never named it. It took Lee's look of horror to understand that what had happened wasn't my fault.

Henry took advantage of my intoxicated state, of my inability to hurt his feelings. I'd clung to my own guilt and fear of slut-shaming, but this epiphany broke the load from me.

Since then, I've told three other friends—two of them women. It felt like I was testing the words on my tongue each time. With one friend, I didn't name Henry. I didn't want to change her opinion of him. Protecting him felt like protecting myself, I suppose. I don't want to try to explain why I kept him in my life. After the realization that it was rape, I felt too foolish to go to him and say, "Ten years ago, you raped me, and I can't be friends with you anymore."

I should have. I should have stopped his flirting as soon as it started. I should have been clearer with my boundaries. I should have gone home with Will to keep myself safe. I didn't do any of the right things, and it fucks with me. It feels like a slap in the face of my sex positivity, of my feminism. I'm wiser now. I know what happened. I should confront him and stop trying to save myself from the shame of it all. I should be stronger.

He recently said he was sorry to me. Not specifically for what happened that night, but he admitted he'd been wrong. Wrong to flirt and try to pressure me into sex all these years. I accepted the apology but still didn't bring up what I now know was rape. I still feel like I have to protect us both. I still feel like I would be blamed for flirting, for drinking, for possibly having an orgasm during the assault, for not confronting him sooner, for letting his unwanted innuendos go on for so long.

I'd been so worried about losing his friendship, but time is winning there. We aren't as close as we used to be. He's married now and building his business. We remain in contact, but mainly via social media and a few quick text messages. We share each other's accomplishments through retweets and likes. I think he's recently begun therapy, which is what led to his apology.

Once in a while, a large group of us used to travel for a gathering, usually to a house party for someone's birthday or wedding. Henry would often be there, but not Will. Will detached himself from the group after our messy breakup. The irony is too thick to cut. The one I wanted all those years ago turned into a ghost, and it's the unwanted one who haunts me.

Would Henry understand why it was rape? Would he understand that even with the lack of violence, there was still force, that he took a decision from me? I don't think I will ever talk to him about it. I know what happened. Henry violated a trust. He did something wrong. And what he did has a name, even if I must whisper it.

Bones, Depression, and Me

After staring at the ceiling, trying to figure out if I could will myself to die, I would close my eyes and try to imagine a total blackness. Instead, I would always see images of my mother's face, crying uncontrollably as she went through my belongings to give away. At the time, I would say Los Angeles tried to kill me, but it wasn't really the city. I loved LA. I hope to live there again. But I'd moved there with no real plan, to escape a bad breakup, then got into another relationship too much like the one I was escaping. Both left me with emotional trauma I didn't take time to unpack. I was over thirty, single, and fat, and could barely make ends meet. All of these depression triggers could've happened anywhere, and I later realized they had, but I knew then I needed to leave Los Angeles or else I would die there, one way or another. Seeing my mother's face each time I tried to meditate myself to death seemed like a sign I needed to go home.

But before I could do that, I had a writers' retreat I wanted to attend in Napa Valley. Somehow, I'd convinced myself to give grad school another try, and I'd enrolled in the University of Southern California's then Master of Professional Writing Program. I had an emphasis in poetry. One of my professors also coordinated the poetry division of a weeklong writers' retreat in St. Helena, California. She strongly encouraged me to apply, so I did—with financial aid. My major logistical problem was that I'd already ended my lease with the lady who rented me a room and I couldn't extend it. I needed someplace to stay for the few weeks until the retreat. I felt like I'd already used up all the goodwill I had with my LA friends, so I asked some friends in Las Vegas if I could stay with them, and they welcomed me with open arms.

I put a bunch of my shit in storage and took a bus to Vegas. DL, my friend with the Chicago house parties, and his wife, Chandler, had moved to Sin City and had a gorgeous three-story town house. I slept in a guest room on the third floor with an en suite bathroom. But it was in the second-floor living room where I found major comfort in their Netflix account. All of my DVDs were in storage, so I couldn't do my seasonal binge of *Frasier*. DL was really into having an entertainment system, so their television was as wide as I was tall. Every day I plopped myself on the floor, with my back against the couch, and watched *Bones* until they came home from work.

I'd never seen *Bones* before. A commercial or two had popped up and I'd heard people make jokes about how addictive the show was, but I'd never felt compelled to tune in.

Until I was depressed in Nevada. I grew up on *Perry Mason* and *Columbo* reruns, and *Murder, She Wrote.* The swooning lady in red atop a grave in the opening credits of PBS's *Mystery!* series (now simply *Masterpiece Theatre*) always got me hyped. Murder mysteries and procedurals are my happy place, so I figured I'd put *Bones* on as background noise for my reading, but soon I found myself entranced.

Temperance Brennan (Emily Deschanel), also known as Bones, is a forensic anthropologist who doesn't let emotions get in the way of facts. She's so focused on evidence and logic she has no sense of pop culture or interpersonal social cues, and she does not believe in God. Seeley Booth (David Boreanaz) is an FBI special agent who wears a belt buckle with a rooster that says COCKY on it and color-ful striped socks. An Army Rangers veteran, he loves his country and his Roman Catholic religion, but approaches all cases with warmth and empathy. When Booth comes across a crime scene with skeletal remains, he brings Brennan on the case. She and her team of competent, wacky scien-tists do all the cool forensic stuff with technology, gadgets, science, and art to identify the victim and find out how they died; then she and Booth investigate the living to find out why they killed. She's emotionless. He's a charmer. She's evidence-based. He relies on his gut. She's a pretty woman. He's a good-looking man. Will they…? Won't they…?

Inject it into my veins.

One day, I hit PLAY on season one, episode one. Then I

blinked, and season two was about to start. Somehow I had ripped through twenty-two episodes of a show I'd intended to only halfway pay attention to. Each episode follows a neat formula: a cold open with remains in various stages of grossness; Brennan and her team identify the victim; Brennan and Booth go question surviving family members, coworkers, friends, and/or lovers; the scientists discover how the victim died; Brennan and Booth banter; everyone tries to teach Brennan how to be a human; they solve the case, then grab drinks at a bar or pie at a diner; and we wait for the next episode to see if our two leads will ever see each other naked. The show hardly ever strays from its formula, unless a serial killer shows up to stretch their crimes over a season or more.

The routine of *Bones* saved me from losing my mind entirely. Maybe I could've latched on to any number of procedurals available at that time, but *Bones* became a kind of savior for me. When I watched that show, I knew everything would work out. Something that started as a mess stumbled upon by strangers became a human being who had people fighting to give their story a proper ending. I needed that.

Because I was in the middle of a major depressive period, I watched the show mostly from a place of numbness. I enjoyed it and paid attention, but I hardly ever had an emotional reaction to anything. I could recognize the humor, the sexual tension, the patriotic (read: xenophobic) lessons Booth tried to impart. (*Bones* was a good show, but it wasn't particularly subtle.) If anyone had been watching me during this binge, they would've seen a blank-faced woman staring at the TV, unblinking, moving only to go to the bathroom or grab food. Then I made it to the ninth episode of the second season, and something finally broke inside me.

"Aliens in the Spaceship" introduces the first serial killer of the show via a pair of twins whose remains are found in some kind of capsule. They had been buried alive. The same killer kidnaps Brennan and one of her colleagues, Jack Hodgins (T. J. Thyne), a conspiracy theory–loving entomologist, and buries them in a car underground somewhere, leaving Booth and the rest of the team to try to figure out where they are and how to get to them before they run out of air and die. It's a pretty intense episode. Hodgins admits his love for another of their colleagues, and they both write out final letters for their loved ones, if they don't make it. They're going to try one last daring attempt to blow themselves out of wherever they are, because they're not sure if Booth got the signal they managed to send using their big ole brains and expertise.

Of course, Booth finds them just in time. They've been buried in some kind of sandy construction site. Booth sees the explosion, runs like his own life depends on it, slides down a huge embankment all heroic-like, and begins digging with his bare hands. He pulls out Brennan, and they hug and sigh over each other, and with my butt going numb in the real world, I turned into a blubbering fool.

Did anyone out there love me enough to rescue me? Who would my last thought be of before I slip away? What would my last letters say to the ones I loved? How could I pull myself out of this gritty depression, which was sanding down my real self and making me an emotionless zombie? Did I love myself enough to be my own hero?

That episode fucked me up, and I still go back to it when I need a good cry.

They didn't find the killer, and the routine of the show, the most comforting part for me, had been disrupted, derailed by a menacing outside force. The mission was now survival. Without the show's routine, Brennan and Hodgins got to know each other as human beings, not just as colleagues, and Hodgins realized life could be over at any moment so he had to be bold.

I'd had plans, too, and then depression came and sat heavy on my chest. I hadn't yet figured out what was next, but suddenly I knew I wanted to make it out alive. I knew I had people who loved me and who would miss me. I had people I'd yet to meet that I wanted to love.

It didn't matter that Brennan and Booth didn't find the killer then, that there was no neat ending. They'd survived. Sometimes that's all you can promise yourself—that you'll survive—and then the new plan for the next steps will come together.

After I cried over a set of fictional characters I had never particularly related to before, I began to watch the show differently. I could giggle at Hodgins's horny lovesickness. I could admire Booth's broad shoulders and slim hips. I could nod my head to Brennan's frequent and unapologetic acknowledgment of her own worth and expertise. The zombie was gone.

This is not to say *Bones* cured my depression. Absolutely not. By the time I eventually made it back home to Nashville, the amount of emotional energy it took so I wouldn't appear as depressed as I was drained me until I finally ended up crying in my mother's arms. So, no, *Bones* did not make my depression disappear, but it made me realize the fighter in me was still there. I just had to dig her out.

The Life of a Succubus

Men have been crawling on their knees for me for a long time.

When Rocco and I broke up at the beginning of my senior year in high school, he cried. I tried to remain as coolheaded as possible, but I broke down, too. I finally told him to leave, probably because my mom would be home soon. He walked away, head low, tears streaking his face, but he suddenly turned back. He dropped to his knees and crawled to me, begging me not to break up with him. He grabbed me by the waist and pushed his face into my lower belly, sobbing all over me.

We were seventeen. The only thing we knew how to do with any cool was sneak out of the house.

I rolled my eyes at Rocco's dramatics. Too many R&B videos and too much *Boyz n the Hood* had led to this. In the film, Tre's impotent rage after an encounter with police had sent him to Brandi's house, where he fought the air before falling to his knees and crying in her arms, his face pressed to her stomach. The incident led them to make love for the first time. My friends and I would later mock the dramatic moment because Tre had already been such a horndog, constantly trying to get Brandi to stray from her Catholic beliefs. He finally got some sympathy tang.

I shouldn't belittle Rocco's emotions at the time. He may well have truly been devastated by our breakup. We'd talked about going away to college together and getting married, and we were each other's first real relationship. Even though I knew he was acting his little heart out, watching him crawl to me sent a twinge through the right side of my lower belly, the place where instant, powerful arousal hits me. He'd never crawled to me before, and my exposure to porn had never shown men in such a submissive position. Men would be on their knees, sure, but they always maintained power. I didn't know that's what I was experiencing at the time, but I felt a rush of some secret strength. I'd made this man-boy beg.

This is my strongest sexual memory of Rocco.

When I try to trace the history of my need for men on their knees, this is what I think of.

———

As I've mentioned before, my Good Lover Radar™ has a 90 percent accuracy rating, and when I saw Alex in person for the first time, I knew he was filthy and had a big dick. A big dick he knew how to use. That's important. Some men think all you need is meat, but what about the seasoning?

Alex and I met on Okayplayer, where all of us members were supposed to be talking about hip-hop but more often than not, we were flirting and trading insults, music, recipes, and eventually bodily fluids. Alex was short and wiry, strong just the way I like, with 'tweener brown skin and a little Ewok nose. His voice was deep and raspy on the back notes, not quite late-night quiet storm DJ, but you knew he was capable of it. He was witty and fancied himself a writer, so the after-dark phone conversations of our long-distance situationship left my sheets far too warm. He knew what to say and how to say it. Alex was thunder in the bedroom: noisy and roof-rattling.

I would visit Alex in his basement apartment in Chicago. I liked taking black-and-white pictures of him. He gave good profile. With his head between my thighs, he would turn his face in every position he could to make sure he reached every curve. He ate me out like he wanted to coat his entire face with me. One time, I looked down and he looked up at me with wet pussycat eyes, begging me to tell him what a good job he was doing. It made me catch my breath.

Guys look up to gauge your reaction, to see praise on your face, but it's usually about their own egos. This was different. Alex wanted to make sure he was doing a good job because my pleasure wasn't validation; it was his purpose.

Sometimes after a particularly intense session, he'd whisper, "Thank you," and I swear, it melted me, but I wasn't sure how to handle it. I'd never had anyone thank me for letting him come before. Internally, I loved it, but was I supposed to? I told my friends about it, but hesitantly, hoping to use their reactions to figure out how I should respond.

My guy friends would shake their heads and say, "Nah, he shouldn't be doing all that," but then they'd give me assessing looks, trying to figure out what I had done to make a man thank me for sex. My girlfriends would giggle, then get a far-off look in their eyes, perhaps imagining what it would be like to have a man lose himself in such a way.

I knew about BDSM and what a dominatrix was, but I'd never truly explored it. At the time, my porn habits were very basic—heterocentric and formulaic: sloppy blow jobs, cursory cunnilingus, pound pound pound, facial. Men were dominant, with little care for the woman's pleasure, and women were, if not necessarily submissive, largely passive, accepting what was being done to them with fake moans and ruined mascara.

I may have been considered aggressive—I've always tried to be direct and clear about what I want sexually—but in the bedroom, I loved letting the man be in control...and I loved it when he lost it, shuddering between my thighs or across my tongue.

————

In 2014, it had been over four years since my last relationship, and I was tired of the long stretches without sex. I was worried I didn't know how to be in a relationship anymore, that I'd lost my skills in the bedroom. I wasn't naïve to the hookup nature of online dating, but I also knew that Black women have the lowest reply rate of anyone using these sites or apps. So when I finally activated an OkCupid account that spring, I didn't expect so many white men to reach out to me, or for them to move so quickly into revealing their fetish for Black women. One guy even referred to me as an "ebony girl," as if I belonged in a tag on a porn site.

ME: It's cool you're open to new experiences but I don't know if I can give you what you want

HIM: I think you can. I've never been with an ebony girl before. & you know the saying once you go black you never go back? Lol I'm curious if it's really that good. Is there any truth to that?

ME: Ok. You'll definitely have to find someone else to entertain your "ebony girl" fantasies. I definitely can't help you out there. Best of luck!

I largely ignored the men asking me to dominate them, which happened as frequently as every third or fourth message, but they did make me wonder: Were these men simply casting out a large net, or was there something about me that served as a beacon to white male submissives? Or was it simply enough that I was a Black woman?

As I headed into my late thirties, I thought of all the opportunities of sexual exploration I'd been denied because it may have interfered with an ex's "manhood," or because of my own lack of confidence. I frequently had held myself back from approaching white men, because I didn't think they'd be attracted to me physically or because of cultural differences. Yet here they were presenting themselves to me—even if I had to weed out the creeps. It would be foolish to continue to deny myself. I remembered the surprising thrill I'd felt when Rocco crawled on his knees and begged me to stay together, when Alex looked up at me, the lower part of his face shining, and thanked me for coming in his mouth.

All of this coincided with my decision to make 2014 the year of new adventures, and to stop being afraid of taking chances. So when I received a message from a white man in his early twenties asking if I wanted deep conversation or a sub, I decided to say fuck it and go for it.

After a few messages, I gave him my Google Voice number, and we began texting. In my mind, I started to call him Baby Sub, because it became clear that he, too, was exploring. I made him call me "ma'am" or Miss Q (I won't reveal the name). I knew a little bit of the language used in the D/s community from erotica and eavesdropping on Twitter conversations, but sometimes he'd reply with a term that left me Googling. One time, he told me he liked to watch JOI porn. After a quick search, I discovered the world of "jerk off instruction." I'd later use the genre as a tool to punish him.

After a week or two of texting, we met in person at a café. Close-cropped, wavy strawberry-blond hair framed a face that made me second-guess his age and whether or not I could go through with whatever was about to happen. I checked his ID. He was old enough to drink, but the double-digit age gap between us still left me wary. He was visibly relieved to see me yet also nervous. When I made him go into the restroom and change into a pair of my panties, he stumbled. He modeled the underwear as best he could in a public setting, and there was no doubt about his state of arousal. He liked to be humiliated. He went to work wearing the panties that same day and frequently texted me his thanks. Seeing him in the bikinis did nothing for me, but making him wear them gave me a rush. I wondered what else I could get away with.

ME: Why did you reach out to me? Why did you offer yourself to me?

HIM: You looked really lovely and I decided to take a chance.

Further prodding revealed he had explored some sub behavior with another older Black woman. He liked the maturity of Black women and how we don't put up with a lot of bullshit. He said white women his age were vapid and frequently dismissed him because of his youthful appearance. I didn't feel threatened by his ignorance, even though his desire for a Strong Black Woman to take control of him sexually was an echo of other messages. I wanted to test the limits of my sexuality, so I let it slide.

As my relationship with Baby Sub progressed, I was surprised at how easily some domme behavior came to me. Small things, like forbidding him from interrupting me while I talked, were thrilling. I made sure never to punish in anger, but being able to express my anger was exciting, as was his fear of it—and I didn't have to worry about him passive-aggressively punishing me by hanging out all night with his friends or flirting with other women, or even cheating.

In previous relationships, I could be aggressive in the bedroom, usually with the purpose of getting the guy I was with to ramp up his own aggression. But there were limits. I was expected to be the only one willing to experiment sexually, so whenever I expressed a desire to do something basic like tie up my partner or blindfold him, I was met with resistance. That led to discussions about masculinity, not to mention straight-up fear. My then boyfriends couldn't trust me enough to respect their boundaries. The thought that I might do "butt stuff" to them while they were tied up was too much for them to bear.

Still, when I told my male friends about what was happening in my sex life, they weren't surprised. In fact, one friend was shocked it had taken me so long to get to that point. My love of men on their knees is no secret among my friends. And neither is my sexual appetite. My love for receiving head and wanting sex as much as I can get it are favorite subjects of mine. Add being a feminist and my love for Wonder Woman, a character somewhat created from kink, into the mix, and I guess my guy friends figured I would've donned the latex and leather a while ago.

But even with Baby Sub, I never wore the expected leather-and-latex uniform of a dominatrix. Instead, I shaped my previous experience as an educator into my domme persona.

Baby Sub texted me precisely at the time I'd given him. He told me he'd been to his classes that day and needed to study for a test. He was using flash cards to help him learn musical terms. I told him to clean up. I was coming over to help him study.

When he opened the door, his hair was still wet from the shower. His face was flushed. He was excited to see me and had barely finished greeting me ("Thank you for coming to my apartment, ma'am") before he asked how *I would help him study. I reminded him he was not allowed to question me, and then I led him to his bedroom. He had a couple of textbooks and some handmade flash cards on his bed. As soon as we crossed the threshold into his room, away from the curious eyes of his roommates, he assumed the position: on his knees, head down, hands behind his back. Good boy.*

I looked at the flash cards. Words and phrases on the front, definitions and explanations on the back. I walked behind him, still on his knees, and ran my hand along his shoulders. He let out a sigh. I pulled his head back roughly, then leaned close to his ear and spoke softly: "I'm going to get in the bed. Once I'm settled, you may get in the bed. Stay at the foot, on your knees, just like this. I'm going to read a term and you tell me the definition. For each one you get right, I'll let you service me for ten minutes. For each one you get wrong, I'll subtract ten minutes. Is that clear?"

"Yes, Mistress."

"That's a good pet."

I made Baby Sub grow his hair out so I could have something to pull. I put him on masturbation restriction. He wasn't allowed to touch himself unless I gave him permission. When he had too many typos in his texts, I made him call me and repeat an apology, which included calling himself too horny to type properly, until I told him to stop. He had a journal where he had to answer questions I posed. Sometimes I made him watch his favorite kind of porn, knowing he wouldn't be able to give himself any relief. I did not allow any race play, and I would penalize him when he'd say something ignorant about his experiences with Black people, like when he'd disparage the significance of marching bands within HBCU culture, belittling what he saw as a lack of musicality. After a while, it was clear he was bringing up racially sensitive subjects to bait me into punishing him, which led me to forbidding discussions about race.

He was a bratty sub, who frequently tried to exert control by doing things he knew would require punishment or trying to manipulate me to get out of punishments, something called "topping from the bottom." I hated it. It magnified how young he was. And I preferred rewarding him with praise and permission to touch me, rather than punishing him. He wanted to be spanked and insulted, so he would push until I had no choice but to retaliate. To stop his bratty behavior, I put him on time-out: I refused any contact with him. He couldn't see me. No phone calls. No texts. He wasn't allowed to service me. It left him without order, without purpose.

Despite all of this, I still felt like I had no idea what I was doing—but I was learning. I watched videos online, joined FetLife, found a mentor through Twitter, and asked questions. Nashville has a strong underground D/s and swinging culture, but the more I researched, the more I knew I'd never join any clubs or ask to be invited as a guest to explore my options. Through FetLife, I learned that the local men who were masters or dominants were almost all white, and the language in their profiles frequently set off my internal racist alarms. I saw one man with a picture of a Confederate flag belt buckle he used for flogging. The most popular local club, or "professional dungeon," lists in its code of conduct that "respect should always be accorded to every individual," but when I'd see the expected attendees for gatherings, I'd cringe at how few people of color seemed to be present. There were some Black men who were doms, but based on their profiles, they were masters of primarily white women. I didn't feel like I'd be safe or respected if I tried to attend one of the gatherings—not as someone new to the life, and definitely not as a Black woman.

I tried to find local Black women dommes, but the majority of the Black women I found were subs and slaves, who subjected themselves to race play—being called "nigger," or acting as maids or breeders. The few dommes I did see were fairly hardcore, their profiles filled with images of them in latex and stacked heels, whips gleaming in their hands. I was too intimidated to approach them for mentorship. And I knew that wasn't the kind of domme I wanted to be.

So I lived online, researching how to handle male subs.

I asked my male friends to tell me ways they'd like to be punished, if they would allow themselves the freedom of being submissive. Because that's one of the many things I'd discovered as my relationship with Baby Sub continued: All he had to do was wait for me to give him instructions, wait to serve. There's something very freeing about that. Meanwhile, I had to put him on a schedule: when to wake up, when to contact me, when to go to bed. I had to tell him what to wear, distribute punishments and rewards, figure out ways he could be of service. Imagine being a teacher and creating lesson plans, then grading all day, every day, without break. It was slightly exhausting; his need to be controlled was controlling me. Being someone's mistress was more work than I'd anticipated, and I was no longer sure it was sustainable.

In fact, I started to feel more like his mother than his domme. It reminded me a bit of those hetero relationships where the man conveniently acts helpless so the woman has to do everything at home. I resented having to chart out every moment of his life, especially considering I was still figuring out my own. He was trying to steer me into a 24/7 total power exchange, and I didn't want that responsibility. I resented that yet another man, despite his claim of submissiveness, was trying to manipulate me.

Soon our schedules were in conflict, and seeing each other became a chore. He began to throw more tantrums, upset at the lack of time we were spending together. My knee-jerk reaction, habit from my more traditional relationships, was to give him what he wanted. Then I'd remember, *I'm the domme here, not this pouty brat who needs more attention than I can give.* I didn't have to put up with his attempts to manipulate me. So I told him to move on and find someone more willing to devote the time he clearly needed.

Since then, I've had relationships that followed more traditional gender roles, but playing a domme unleashed parts of myself that can't be bottled up again. I'm much more confident voicing displeasure, as well as satisfaction. I've also learned that when people call it a lifestyle, they really mean it. It's so much more than tying someone up or wanting to be spanked. It can consume you, but it's also a responsibility.

When I moved to New York in 2017, I was still lurking at FetLife, but I couldn't see myself pursuing domme life more seriously. My Twitter mentor told me I'm horrible at establishing boundaries, and she was right. Baby Sub and I sometimes hung out in public, giving the appearance that we were a "real couple," and letting Baby Sub think he had a more significant status than he actually did. It was a rookie mistake.

I deactivated my OkCupid account, feeling like it had served its purpose. I haven't talked to Baby Sub in years. I joined Feeld, which is hailed as the kinky dating app, and I've had quite a few good times as a result. I don't think I can ever get enough of having men come to my home, remain silent, eat me out as long as I want, and then leave without any expectation of reciprocity. It truly makes me feel like a goddess.

In the language of the community, I'm a switch—someone who can be dominant or submissive, depending on the need.

I want to be worshipped; then I want him to pull my hair. Sometimes I want to beg *please*, but even as I make my voice go all baby girl, I know I still have the power to make him lose himself from a few breathy words. And when he is no longer in control because of something I said against his ear or because I hiked my leg around his waist, it fills me up so much I can feel myself glowing inside. Dominant, submissive, mistress or baby girl, the power always returns to me.

Acknowledgments

When I would visit home, after moving away and finding myself stuck in a practical career I hated, my aunt Gwen would ask me, "Nicki, when are you writing a book? Where's your book, Nick?" Here it is, Gwen. Thank you.

Mama, I bring you into everything I do because a love like yours should be immortalized, and I want everyone to know there is no me without you.

To my sister and brother: I love y'all beyond thought. I'm so thankful I have you on either side of me to keep me standing.

For my father: I know you tried. I'm trying, too.

Thank you to everyone at the 2017 BuzzFeed Emerging Writers fellowship program—the editors and my cohort—Jennifer H. Choi, Alessa Dominguez, and Frederick McKindra. You helped me realize this book was possible.

Kima Jones and the 2017 Jack Jones Retreat were such a

blessing to me. I shared one of the first chapters I'd written for this book at the retreat and met some incredible writers there. Take me back to New Mexico!

I don't know how to thank my agent Kiele Raymond or my editor Maddie Caldwell enough. I missed so many deadlines! But you both stuck with me and made me feel like I was writing something worthwhile.

Thank you to my copy editors, to Jacqueline Young, and to the cover artist, Adriana Bellet, and everyone else at Grand Central Publishing who helped get this book into readers' hands.

My beta readers! Thank you so much for taking time out of your busy schedules to give me helpful feedback. I was so worried that I'd written something only I could under-stand, and you assured me that was not the case. Kalenda Eaton, Cynthia Harris, Danny Lavery, Al Letson, and Rashad Mobley, you are all golden shimmers in my life.

Cynthia, you gave me the push I needed to write a certain chapter, and I'm glad you did. You have been there to witness the moment when I started to believe in my own magic. I don't know if there is such a thing as a Bad Bitch Doula, but that's what you are.

Michael Arceneaux, Keah Brown, Ashley C. Ford, Roxane Gay, Saeed Jones, R. Eric Thomas, Jesmyn Ward—your work has cleared a path for me, and I am forever grateful.

Bim Adewunmi, Alisha Cheek, Tracy Clayton, Dria Roland…I'm so proud of each of you. Y'all know how I hate the mushiness, but I have learned so much from each of you, and I am ready to be a part of your World Domination Committees. Please put me in charge of the skinny men.

Nicole Cliffe! You know what you'd done for me, and I think you're incredible.

Keisha Dutes, Julia Furlan, Eleanor Kagan, Neena Pathak, Cher Vincent…you showed me I can be good at more than what I thought possible. You have changed my life. Thank you.

To all the Thirst Buckets out there…I was hosting Thirst Aid Kit while working on this book, and sharing those thirsty moments with you often helped me stay sane. Sometimes I would think that my work was insignificant, but you'd send a thoughtful email or a shamelessly parched tweet, and turn my thoughts around. You are a true joy in my life, and I miss you.

If you do not see your name here or any mention of you in the book, please do not take it personally. Maybe you'll show up in the next memoir or I'll write a fictionalized version of you into something else. I finished this book during a pandemic, and it was very stressful!

If any of the men I wrote about read this and want to talk, you can find me wherever you get your podcasts…but don't.

Reading Group Guide

Discussion Questions

1. In "Fast," how does Nichole see and feel that intimacy is a double-edged sword often turned against women? How has sex and desire shaped your life in terms of these dueling capacities?

2. In "A Woman Who Shouts," how does Nichole negotiate her relationship with religion alongside the pressures of societal expectations and the judgment of the congregations she's a part of? What does this say about how we each can navigate the world when faced with external pressures?

3. It took growing up for Nichole to recognize the abusive qualities of Kermit and Miss Piggy's relationship. Reflecting on the pop culture you consumed as a child, what subliminal or explicit messaging do you think was passed on to you at an early age?

4. Nichole reflects on a number of past romantic relationships in the essay "White Boys." Several of them taught her valuable lessons about what she is willing to put up with (or not), particularly as she experienced several racist incidents. How do these experiences speak to the difficulties and complexities of dating as a Black woman? What does that reveal about the prevalence of racism, and the failure of white allyship, in America more broadly?

5. Janet Jackson's career and her public perception left lasting impressions on both Nichole and her mother, albeit very different ones. How is it possible that we each draw such disparate meanings? About her body, Nichole writes that "everyone saw what they wanted to see." Could that be true of these pop culture artifacts as well?

6. In "Prince's Girl," Nichole writes that the titular artist was a "stranger [she] knew [she'd] never meet, but he knew [her]." What is so meaningful about feeling recognized or represented in the media we consume? How does this essay and the larger collection speak to the effects of a dearth of positive Black representation in pop culture?

7. Both with Hector and in reference to the Okayplayer message boards, Nichole explores the value of boundaries. Especially now, as the internet has become integral to every facet of our lives, why is it important to construct

boundaries and determine limits? Likewise, how are they important in our real-life relationships?

8. Nichole says she finds power in a range of roles, from dominant to submissive, mistress to baby girl. What do you think is empowering about exploring such dynamics within sexuality generally and for women specifically? What restrictions are placed on the sexuality of Black women in particular that might complicate these power dynamics?

9. The popularity of true and fictionalized crime shows, podcasts, and books continues to grow, as Nichole illustrates on a micro level with the show *Bones*. What do you think attracted her to that show during a particularly dark period of her life? What do you think this says about our collective interest in crime?

10. In a number of her essays, Nichole touches on the importance of being seen in pop culture. Feeling seen by people, like her college classmates or Aunt C, seems to have made an equally significant impact on Nichole. Do you have anyone you think shaped the course of your life or sense of self in this way?

11. Nichole focuses on a number of pop culture touchstones throughout this collection, from *Cheers* to Prince,

analyzing how they shaped her understanding of the world. What are a few cultural touchstones that likewise affected how you interact with our society and culture more broadly?

12. The title of the book is a line from "If I Was Your Girlfriend," Nichole's favorite Prince song, referenced in the chapter "Prince's Girl." Although she does not explicitly quote this line in her memoir, how do you think it represents the theme of the book and Nichole's life overall?

About the Author

Nichole Perkins is a writer from Nashville, Tennessee. She is a 2017 Audre Lorde Fellow at the inaugural Jack Jones Literary Arts Retreat and a 2017 BuzzFeed Emerging Writers Fellow. She is also a 2016 Callaloo Creative Writing Fellow for poetry. Nichole currently hosts *This Is Good For You,* a podcast about the ways we seek pleasure in life. She formerly co-hosted *Thirst Aid Kit,* a podcast about pop culture and desire, and was also a co-host of *The Waves* podcast at Slate, which looked at news and culture through a feminist lens. Her first collection of poetry, *Lilith, but Dark,* was published by Publishing Genius in July 2018.